SACRED JOURNEYS

SACRED
JOURNEYS

Your Guide to the World's Most
Transformative Spaces,
Places, and Sites

Meera Lester

Adams Media
New York London Toronto Sydney New Delhi

Adams Media
An Imprint of Simon & Schuster, Inc.
57 Littlefield Street
Avon, Massachusetts 02322

Copyright © 2019 by Simon & Schuster, Inc.

First Adams Media trade paperback edition
January 2019

ADAMS MEDIA and colophon are
trademarks of Simon & Schuster.

For information about special discounts
for bulk purchases, please contact Simon &
Schuster Special Sales at 1-866-506-1949
or business@simonandschuster.com.

The Simon & Schuster Speakers Bureau can
bring authors to your live event. For more
information or to book an event contact
the Simon & Schuster Speakers Bureau at
1-866-248-3049 or visit our website at
www.simonspeakers.com.

Interior design by Stephanie Hannus
Interior images © Getty Images

Manufactured in the United States of America

10 9 8 7 6 5 4 3 2 1

Library of Congress Cataloging-in-
Publication Data has been applied for.

ISBN 978-1-72140-019-5
ISBN 978-1-72140-020-1 (ebook)

Scriptural passages from the Bible quoted
in this book are taken from King James Holy
Bible, Old and New Testaments; translated
out of the original tongues; and with the
former translations diligently compared and
revised by His Majesty's special command.
Appointed to be read in churches.
Oxford University Press, Publication—no
date. London; Oxford University Press,
Publication—no date; Amen Corner, New
York: 35 West 32nd Street.

Contains material adapted from the
following title published by Adams Media,
an Imprint of Simon & Schuster, Inc.: *Sacred
Travels* by Meera Lester, copyright © 2011,
ISBN 978-1-4405-2489-9.

CONTENTS

INTRODUCTION

H umans have long sought sacred places to express their faith, find meaning, gain guidance, receive healing, mourn a loss, and experience renewal. From Mecca to the energy vortexes of Sedona, Arizona, and from the sacred stones of Stonehenge in England to Crater Lake in the Cascade Mountains of Oregon, these hallowed places are as varied as the people who visit them.

These mystical environments, which are often associated with mysterious energies or special powers, can serve as oases for an arid heart or lift a spiritually yearning soul. In sacred places, you can engage in a rite of passage, light a ceremonial candle, meditate, pay homage to your ancestors, or simply offer a few words of gratitude to the people or forces of nature that created such a wonder.

This book is your guide to two hundred sacred places throughout the world. These transformative sites range from hidden grottoes, natural springs, red-colored cliffs, and ancient stone circles to vaulted-ceilinged cathedrals, massive megaliths, stone pyramids, intricately carved temples, and totems. There are even entire towns, mountain ranges, seemingly endless rivers, ancient forests, and Iron Age ring forts that are considered sacred in some traditions.

Your spiritual journey can take you all over the world. On the following pages, you'll find different icons for the geographic location where each destination is found:

Asia	*
Europe	^
North America	~
South America	#
Africa	+
Oceania	%

Explore your spirituality. Visit one or more of the many sacred sites in the world to pay respect, meditate, reflect, perform a ritual, or follow the ancient cycle of prayer—that is, praise, worship, and listen. Then let inspiration guide you into action. Repeat the cycle, inspired by the spirits of the sacred places you visit.

Acropolis of Baalbek
(also Romanized Triad of Heliopolis)✪
Baalbek, Lebanon

Love is all we have, the only way that each can help the other.
—Euripides (ca. 480–406 B.C.), Greek playwright

A fter Alexander the Great conquered and Hellenized Baalbek, changing its name to Heliopolis, the Romans assimilated their deities Jupiter, Mercury, and Venus with the indigenous deities Baal (Lord), Aliyan (Baal's son), and Anat (Baal's daughter and Aliyan's consort). Then, on a hilltop in Heliopolis, the Romans spent two hundred years building the Acropolis of Baalbek—one of the largest and finest temple complexes of the Greco-Roman period. For centuries, people worshipped at the monument and at the round Temple of Venus, goddess of love and tutelary deity of the acropolis.

If you wish to safeguard your love or to contemplate religious tolerance, journey to Baalbek. The best way to tour this World Heritage site is with a local guide. Baalbek is a major town in eastern Lebanon, accessible by road from Beirut (nearest airport) and Damascus, Syria.

Soothe Your Spirit

Bring a small stone symbolizing romantic love (red, heart-shaped) or Divine love (white, thunderbolt-shaped). Carry your love talisman as you stroll around the site, soaking in the sacred power of this former city of love and grace.

A Deeper Look

In 1200 B.C., long before the Romans arrived, the Canaanites built a sanctuary here, where they honored Astarte, goddess of love and fertility. Archaeologists believe that the Assyrians, Phoenicians, and Israelites may have also worshipped at this site.

Agii Apostoli (Church of the Holy Apostles) Solaki◐
Athens, Attica, Greece

Give me where to stand, and I will move the earth.
—Archimedes (ca. 287–212 B.C.), Greek mathematician and intuitive

This Byzantine church stands below the ancient Acropolis of Athens and along the agora (open-air place of assembly), where saints, philosophers, and orators imparted their ideology and insights to all within earshot. The rose-colored brick exterior features lovely crenulated arches over narrow wooden doors and a heavy metal bell hanging from a large protruding stone (as no bell tower exists) as well as white stone benches in the courtyard. Inside, ornate Corinthian columns support the arches of a dome adorned with frescoes of cherubs, angels, John the Baptist, and the Christ Pantocrator (Almighty, or Sustainer of the World).

Whether you seek spiritual sustenance or enlightenment, include this lovely church in your visit to Athens. Agii Apostoli Solaki, in the heart of the city, is best seen on foot. Entrance is free.

Soothe Your Spirit

Take refuge from the sun's heat and your racing thoughts in the church's cool, calm interior. Standing under the dome's frescoes, pray for the assurance or guidance you seek. Before continuing your exploration of Athens, sit on one of the outside benches and reflect on the sacred message sent to your heart by the apostles, or perhaps Christ Pantocrator.

A Deeper Look

The church was built in the tenth century A.D. over a second-century nymphaion (sacred spring) honoring nymphs, the nurturing water deities of Greek mythology.

Ajanta Caves✷
Ajanta, Maharashtra, India

Be a lamp unto yourself. Work out your liberation with diligence.
—Siddhartha Gautama, the Buddha (563–483 B.C.), father of Buddhism

O n the cliff of a deep forest ravine overlooking the Waghora River in the Sahyadri Hills of southern India is a sacred treasure: twenty-nine rock-cut caves used as Buddhist monasteries and temples from the second century B.C. to the seventh century A.D. The tenacity it took to chisel these monuments out of volcanic rock is testament to spiritual devotion. The beauty of the friezes of the Buddha and bodhisattvas adorning the walls and ceilings of the caves speaks to the liberating light of such devotion.

If you want to clear your mind of worldly woes and open your heart for inner guidance, visit the Ajanta Caves. Fly into Mumbai (international airport) or Aurangabad (domestic airport). From Aurangabad, take a coach tour, bus, rental car, hired driver/car, or taxi to the caves, which are about an hour away. The caves are open 9:00 a.m. to 5:30 p.m. Tuesday through Sunday and are closed Mondays.

Soothe Your Spirit
Explore the caves mindfully, absorbing the beauty and serenity of this holy place. Focus on your breath, exhaling the stale air of doubt, inhaling the fresh air of knowing.

A Deeper Look
Around A.D. 650, the monks abandoned their Ajanta sanctuary in favor of the Ellora Caves, 62 miles away. The Ajanta Caves faded into obscurity until they were rediscovered in 1819 by a British hunting party that chased a tiger into one of the caves.

Al-Aqsa Mosque✱

Jerusalem, Israel

A good word is like a good tree whose root
is firmly fixed and whose top is in the sky.
—Qur'an, 14–Ibrahim

Al-Aqsa, the second-oldest and third–most sacred mosque in Islam, stands on a holy site of prayer once occupied by the Crusaders and later by the Knights Templar. Built in A.D. 1033 after an earthquake demolished the existing mosque, Al-Aqsa is also one of Islam's most important learning and worship centers and the largest mosque in Jerusalem, with the capacity to accommodate five thousand worshippers.

If you seek spiritual guidance or increased knowledge of the Islamic faith, visit this mosque. Located on Temple Mount in Jerusalem's Old City, Al-Aqsa and the Dome of the Rock form the centerpieces of the Noble Sanctuary (Haram al-Sharif), 35 enclosed acres of sacred gardens, fountains, and structures.

Worshippers are expected to ritually purify themselves before entering the mosque. A woman's body and hair must be covered, and men and women pray in separate areas. The mosque's main ablution fountain, al-Kas (the Cup)—situated between the Dome of the Rock and the Al-Aqsa Mosque—has taps and stone benches.

Soothe Your Spirit

Stand attentively, quietly disconnecting from the world, and consider that you are standing in the presence of Allah or God. After the traditional ritual prayer, issue your personal prayer of petition or gratitude.

A Deeper Look

Al-Masjid El-Aqsa in Arabic means "farthest mosque" and alludes to Prophet Muhammad's legendary Night Journey from Mecca to Jerusalem, which the Dome of the Rock venerates.

Al-Aqsa Mosque, Jerusalem, Israel

Ales Stenar (Ale's Stones)⬢
Kåseberga, Sweden

We should build with the stones we have.
—Swedish proverb

This Swedish megalithic monument, an enigma similar to Stonehenge, consists of fifty-nine stones that form the shape of a boat on the green plains of southern Sweden near the fishing village of Kåseberga. Scholars have determined the approximate creation date of the monument was at the end of the Nordic Iron Age or roughly 2,700 years ago. They speculate that the stone formation could have been an ancient burial site, a monument to the Vikings (who believed death was a journey into the unknown), or possibly the earthly stone ship of the god Heimdall of the ancient Scandinavians. The position of this ship on Earth in relation to celestial bodies in heaven has implications for measuring the transit of the sun, cycles of the seasons, and winter and summer solstices.

If you are curious about the spiritual beliefs of the ancient peoples who constructed the megalithic monuments or would value time in quiet reflection in the serene, cool climate of southern Sweden, visit Ales Stenar. There are bed-and-breakfast establishments in Kåseberga and hotels in nearby Ystad. Take bus 322 or drive from Ystad to Kåseberga and then walk from the parking lot uphill to the stones.

Soothe Your Spirit
Read about Ales Stenar in preparation for seeing the monument. As you walk around the monument, reflect on the ancient builders of the megalithic monuments (there are many in Sweden), as well as the Vikings, and what relevance their spiritual beliefs might have for you.

A Deeper Look
The Ales Stenar monument is more than 219 feet long. At the solstices, the ship's bow and stern are aligned to the position of the sun.

Amorgos ◉
Cyclades Islands, Greece

The dream is realized where you do not expect it.
—Greek proverb

A round the Greek island of Amorgos, the royal blue hue of the Aegean Sea shifts to the brilliant turquoise of a Byzantine tile, in stark contrast to the gray-green and ruddy brown vegetation on the island's tallest mountain, Krikelos. Inhabited since prehistoric times, this breathtaking sanctuary stretching more than 20 miles long and almost 4 miles wide has a wild, unrestrained beauty that is quintessentially Greek—inspiring spiritual seekers, poets, lovers, nature buffs, and globe trekkers alike.

If a nature retreat might help you cultivate a more intimate relationship with the Divine or rejuvenate a personal relationship with a lover, friend, or family member, visit Amorgos in the spectacular Cyclades, the most easterly of the Greek Islands. From Piraeus, the port of Athens, take the ferry to Amorgos to either the village of Katapola (in the central and more populous part of the island) or Aigiali (in the north).

Soothe Your Spirit

Make your way to Chora by car, bus, bike, or on foot, depending where you stay on the island. Take a stroll through this bougainvillea-covered village, where you will find many small churches and other quiet places conducive to prayer. When a spot calls to you, bow your head and pray for your relationship needs.

A Deeper Look

The most dazzling feature on Amorgos is the white-washed monastery of Panagia Chozoviotissa, built on a sheer cliff 186 feet above the Aegean.

Anne Frank House●

Amsterdam, Netherlands

How wonderful it is that nobody need wait a single moment before starting to improve the world.
—Anne Frank (1929–1945), German Jewish diarist

When Anne Frank and her family hid to escape Nazi persecution in 1942 in a house at Prinsengracht 267, Anne detailed the isolation and fears of discovery in her diary until her family was betrayed. Anne and her sister, Margot, were sent to the Bergen-Belsen concentration camp, but her father survived and drew spiritual strength from his daughter's diary (now published in seventy languages).

If you feel a spiritual calling to improve the world, visit the Anne Frank House. It is open year-round, except on January 1 when it is open for half the day and on Yom Kippur when it is closed. Take trams 13, 14, or 17 and get off at the Westermarkt stop, or take the bus 170, 172, or 174 to the Westermarkt stop. Also, the Museumboat stops on the canal directly in front of the house. No photography is allowed.

Soothe Your Spirit

Take your time walking through this house, see the original diary, and use what you learn as a lens for gaining a larger perspective about how one person might make a difference to those who have no voice.

A Deeper Look

The house that hid the Frank family dates to 1635, built by Dirk van Delft with the canal-facing facade renovated in 1739.

Apamea ✪
Syria

I have found power in the mysteries of thought.
—Euripides (ca. 480–406 B.C.), Greek playwright

The once glorious Greco-Roman city of Apamea now lies in rubble—except for remnants of the main boulevard and the Cardo Maximus (Grand Colonnade) that ran alongside it—a grand procession of four hundred granite fluted columns connected by lavishly carved granite lintels. Located at a critical Middle Eastern intersection overlooking the verdant Ghab Valley, Apamea was a major center of trade, politics, and religious thought—including Monophysitism (the doctrine that Christ had only one nature, Divine)—from 300 B.C. to A.D. 1157. At its peak, it was home to half a million people and enjoyed a constant flow of visitors (including Cleopatra).

If walking along an ancient road where myriad religious thoughts were examined and sometimes threatened might help you to understand or to strengthen your faith, come to Apamea. Book a tour (several are available in-country; English guidebooks are available), or hire a guide and car in Hama, 35 miles to the south. Women are advised to travel with a male companion or by group tour. Bring bottled water. Dress appropriately for the culture (Muslim), for the climate (hot, dry), and for walking (lots of it).

Soothe Your Spirit
As you walk this sprawling intersection of sacred beliefs, examine your own, staying open to whatever Divine truths are whispered on the wind.

A Deeper Look
Human occupation at this site dates to the Stone Age and extends to the Middle Ages. During the Christian period, Saint Paul (Saul before his conversion on the road to Damascus) passed through Apamea (then Phrygia).

Aradhana Gala (Meditation Rock) ✪
Mihintale, Sri Lanka

You cannot travel the path until you have become the path itself.
—Siddhartha Gautama, the Buddha, (563–483 B.C.), father of Buddhism

When Indian Emperor Ashoka wanted to spread Buddhism, he sent his son Mahinda with yellow-robed Buddhist monks to the island of Sri Lanka on the full moon of June 247 B.C. While camping on the sacred mountain of Mihintale, they encountered King Devanampiya Tissa and gave him a sapling from the bodhi tree of the Buddha's enlightenment. Today, Mihintale is considered the cradle of Sri Lankan Buddhism, and meditation on the holy peak under the full moon in June is a popular pilgrimage.

If climbing a sacred mountain with a meditation rock on its peak and amazing panoramic views is the kind of pilgrimage that speaks to your spiritual yearning, come to Aradhana Gala in Mihintale. Get there early and give yourself plenty of time to walk the site and climb the 1,840 granite steps. The mountain is about 5 miles from the bus depot of Anuradhapura, the nearest city.

Soothe Your Spirit
Carry the words of Buddha in your heart as you explore the upper terrace; then remove your shoes and climb to the white Maha Seya dagoba (said to house a single hair and some ashes of the Buddha) before venturing up to the meditation rock and even beyond to the seated Buddha. Find a place to meditate, if only for a few moments—there are a couple of stone meditation slabs overlooking a pond and the mountains.

A Deeper Look
When Mahinda first introduced Buddhism to Sri Lanka, Buddhist monks at Mihintale would take refuge and meditate in caves during the rainy season.

Avebury Henge⬡

Avebury, Wiltshire County, England

*Some keep the Sabbath going to Church— / I keep it, staying at Home— /
With a Bobolink for a Chorister— / And an Orchard, for a Dome.*
—Emily Dickinson (1830–1886), American poet

Roughly 4,500 years ago, Neolithic people formed a community in what is now the lovely farming village of Avebury in southern England, constructing massive megalithic monuments and a stone circle 1,401 feet in diameter and covering 28 acres. Today, the site is important for its archaeological and anthropological information as well as for its enigmatic and spiritual properties. It is especially venerated by modern Earth-based spiritual traditions, such as Wicca and neo-Druidism, whose rituals often involve stone circles from which to draw spiritual strength and succor.

If you feel spiritually aligned in natural settings or are intrigued by stone circles and megaliths, visit Avebury Henge—90 miles west of London and 20 miles north of Stonehenge. From London, take a coach tour to Avebury, Stonehenge, and other mysterious sites. From Bath, go by car, bus, or train.

Soothe Your Spirit

Draw in energy as you walk the circle. Holding a crystal pendulum, begin asking questions for guidance—a clockwise-swinging pendulum means yes; counterclockwise means no.

A Deeper Look

Avebury's stone circles consist of an outer ring of ninety-eight slabs of sarsen (the sedimentary rock found in the region) and two inner rings comprised of thirty stones each. This World Heritage site is protected by Britain's National Trust.

Bahá'í House of Worship●
Wilmette, Illinois, United States

O God, guide me, protect me, make of me a shining lamp and a brilliant star...
—Àbdu'l-Bahá (1844–1921), Persian theologian and eldest son of Bahá'u'lláh (founder of the Bahá'í faith)

Like the other eight Bahá'í Houses of Worship in the world, this temple's beauty is circular, has nine sides, and is surrounded by expansive gardens with walkways. Yet, like each of the others, it has its own distinctive—and breathtaking—design. Lacy claddings of ornamental white portland cement cover the exterior and interior walls, columns, and the ceiling of the dome rising 135 feet above the auditorium. Per Bahá'í tenets, the temple welcomes people of all faiths and is used exclusively for worship and learning; no sermons are allowed.

To learn about Bahá'í principles or to worship in a place of tranquil beauty, visit the Bahá'í House of Worship in Wilmette, along Lake Michigan outside Chicago.

Soothe Your Spirit
Sit with your eyes closed and meditate on the Bahá'í belief that we all are of the same God who desires for us to become a unified, egalitarian global society.

A Deeper Look
Founded in Iran in 1844, Bahá'í is the youngest monotheistic religion and today has more than five million adherents. The "Mother Temple of the West" in Wilmette, built from 1920 to 1953, is the oldest surviving temple. The first, built during the years 1902 to 1908 in Turkmenistan, was destroyed in 1948. The other temples are in Australia, Cambodia, Chile, Germany, India, Panama, Samoa, and Uganda.

Banteay Srei ❁

Angkor Wat, Siem Reap, Cambodia

Because thou are All-beauty and All-bliss, / My soul blind and enamoured yearns for Thee...
—Sri Aurobindo (1872–1950), Indian yogi and poet

This tenth-century, red sandstone temple in the massive Angkor Wat temple complex is consecrated to the Hindu deity Shiva, god of destruction. However, it is lovingly called Banteay Srei (Citadel of Women) in reference to the temple's abundance of delicately carved sacred feminine imagery, including Sita (goddess of purity and loyalty, an incarnation of Lakshmi, goddess of prosperity); rosettes; lotuses; and *devatas* and *apsaras*, or dancing nymphs used by the gods to seduce ascetics, demons, and heroes to do their bidding.

If your spiritual practice could use the blessings of loyalty or sacred seduction, visit this temple of war and love, south of the main temple complex of Angkor Thom. A guided tour that includes transportation is the easiest way to visit Banteay Srei (also, Srey). Otherwise, from Phnom Penh take a bus, flight, taxi, or boat (across Tonle Sap Lake) to Siem Reap.

Soothe Your Spirit

Steep your spirit in the subtle sacred energy described by some as Goddess energy in this ancient intricately carved temple. Issue a silent plea for the love, friendship, passion, or compassion you seek.

A Deeper Look

Surrounded by a moat, Banteay Srei has been praised as the precious "jewel of Khmer art" for the exquisite and amazingly well-preserved decorative carvings covering almost every inch of its red (the color of love/passion) sandstone walls.

Banteay Srei, Angkor Wat, Siem Reap, Cambodia

Bardsey Island (Ynys Enlli)◉
Gwynedd, Wales

The Lord is nigh unto them that are of a broken heart;
and saveth such as be of a contrite spirit.
—Bible, Psalm 34:18

A t the tip of the Llŷn Peninsula in North Wales lies a desolate, windswept island a mile long and 0.6 miles across that becomes virtually unreach-able in treacherous sea currents. Nevertheless, it served as a sacred haven for devoutly religious monks and persecuted Christians during the fifth century. Legend holds that the island is also the burial site of King Arthur. All that re-mains of the thirteenth-century monastery and gardens built by Saint Cadfan are the ruins, a tower, and a knobby old Bardsey apple tree that some say the monks planted.

If you are brokenhearted and want to keep a memory alive or see new be-ginnings from loss or departure, visit Bardsey Island. Summer is best. Catch a ferry or a boat from Porth Meudwy or the main market town Pwllheli (mar-ket day is Wednesday) on mainland Wales, where the Cambrian Railway from Shrewsbury in Shropshire, England, clacks past the scenic Cambrian Moun-tains and the coast to its terminus. You can't bring your dogs or other pets, swimming in the sea is not recommended, and visitors are encouraged to en-joy the wildlife but not disturb it.

Soothe Your Spirit

Stay in a farmhouse and give the site time to reinvigorate your spirit as you pray and reflect on how death and destruction can give rise to regeneration and renewal in the cycles of nature and also in human civilization.

A Deeper Look

The Book of Llandaff, assembled in the mid-1200s, noted Bardsey Island as a burial site for twenty thousand "holy confessors and martyrs" and called it the "Rome of Britain" for its sanctity and dignity.

Basílica de Nuestra Señora de Guadalupe
(Basilica of Our Lady of Guadalupe)◕
Mexico City, Mexico

So your strength is failing you?...Mother!
Call her with a loud voice. She is listening to you...
—Saint Josemaría Escrivá (1902–1975), Spanish Roman
Catholic priest and founder of Opus Dei

One of the holiest places in the Western Hemisphere—the Basilica of Our Lady of Guadalupe—might not exist if it weren't for an Aztec peasant. Juan Diego, a newly converted Christian, went to his bishop in Mexico City to request a church be built at Tepeyac, where he had seen an apparition of Virgin Mary. He was told that a heavenly sign was needed. The Virgin made roses bloom in the snow and told Juan to wrap them in his *tilma* (cloak) and take them to the bishop. When Juan delivered the gift, the tilma was miraculously imprinted with an image of the Virgin. That miracle of faith continues to give strength to the church community of the Basilica of Our Lady of Guadalupe.

If you wish to strengthen your spiritual bonds or to see the miraculous cloth, travel to the basilica. The church is located in the Villa de Guadalupe Hidalgo area of Mexico City. Travel by metro to La Villa Station, and then walk two blocks to the church.

Soothe Your Spirit
Light a candle and pray in thanksgiving to Mary for the faith that sustains you and your church community.

A Deeper Look
Digital technology reveals that the image reflected in the Virgin's eyes on the tilma is of the bishop receiving the roses.

Basílica de Nuestra Señora de Guadalupe (Basilica of Our Lady of Guadalupe), Mexico City, Mexico

Basílica de Nuestra Señora de La Altagracia (Higüey Basilica)◉

Salvaleón de Higüey, Dominican Republic

Men do not fear a powerful hostile army as the powers of hell fear the name and protection of Mary.
—Saint Bonaventure (1221–1274), Italian medieval scholastic theologian, philosopher, and Doctor of the Church

In 1502, the Trejo brothers came from Spain to the island of Hispaniola, bringing with them a painting of *La Virgen de la Altagracia* (Our Virgin of High Grace). After the painting disappeared from their house and miraculously reappeared in an orange tree, they erected a chapel at the place of the tree. Today, an elaborate frame holds the painting, now enshrined above the altar of a basilica built in 1972 on the same site. The monolithic Roman Catholic cathedral draws millions of pilgrims and visitors each year, many waiting in long lines to climb the stairs to worship one by one before the icon.

Whether you wish to pray for a loved one's safekeeping or to develop the fierce faith of Mary, come to Higüey Basilica. Two hours from Las Americas International Airport and an hour from Bávaro, the basilica can be reached by public transportation or rental car from anywhere in the country.

Soothe Your Spirit

Place your hand on the icon and pray for the safekeeping you seek. Outside, light an orange candle in gratitude for Mary's holy grace.

A Deeper Look

In 1922, Pope Pius XI crowned Virgin Mary the patron saint of Higüey.

Basilica di San Marco
(Saint Mark's Basilica)◕
Venice, Italy

We are each of us angels with only one wing,
and we can only fly by embracing one another.
—Luciano De Crescenzo (1928–), Italian writer, filmmaker, and engineer

O nce called *Chiesa d'Oro* (Church of Gold) because of its gilded Byzantine mosaics and status as a chapel to the ruling Venetians, this magnificent five-domed Gothic cathedral has long been a symbol of wealth and power. However, the multitudes who flock here to worship or to wed speak more to its holiness and sacred beauty.

Built to safeguard the relics of the Evangelist Saint Mark, Saint Mark's Basilica dominates Piazza San Marco (San Marco Square), where the *Portrait of the Four Tetrarchs* statue anchors the church's southwest corner. Among the basilica's many treasures, the statue represents the interdependence of the four rulers of the Roman Empire.

Whether you wish to sanctify your romantic relationship or your love for the Divine, go to Saint Mark's Basilica. Fly to Venice Marco Polo Airport, and then take a bus, taxi, or ferry to the island.

Soothe Your Spirit

Visit between 11:30 a.m. and 12:45 p.m. if you want to see the mosaics illuminated. Pray with (or for) someone you love.

A Deeper Look

Saint Mark's Basilica, consecrated in A.D. 1094, is the seat of the Venetian archbishop and the third church built on the site. The first was in A.D. 828, when San Marco's body was supposedly found in a pillar in Alexandria and brought to Venice. The golden pillar *Pala d'Oro* is enshrined behind the high altar.

Basilica di Santa Maria degli Angeli (Saint Mary of the Angels)◉
Assisi, Umbria, Italy

Start by doing what's necessary; then what's possible;
and suddenly you are doing the impossible.
—Saint Francis of Assisi (1181–1226), founder of the Franciscans

L ike a heavenly beacon of strength, the gold statue of the Madonna of the Angels ascends from the facade of the blue-domed Basilica of Saint Mary of the Angels, constructed over the ninth-century Porziuncola (small church) where Saint Francis awakened to his ecclesiastical calling. For some, the basilica's splendor and size (the world's seventh-largest Christian church) might seem grandiose, given the saint's vow of poverty, but for those who venerate Saint Francis, it is a fitting homage to this humble servant of God who worked tirelessly for the downtrodden and for animals.

If you want to awaken to your life's purpose or to strengthen your devotion to God, worship at the Basilica di Santa Maria degli Angeli near Assisi, 90 miles from Rome.

Soothe Your Spirit
Reflect on the purity of spirit and inner strength it took for Saint Francis, born into a wealthy noble family, to give away his riches to the poor and to devote his life to Christ and to helping others.

A Deeper Look
A few years after Saint Francis's death in 1226, a simple church was built around the Porziuncola. In 1569, the majestic Gothic basilica was built on top of the smaller (lower) church, and its cupola was positioned directly above the Porziuncola.

Basilica di Santa Maria del Fiore (Duomo)◖
Florence, Italy

The soul that can speak through the eyes, can also kiss with a gaze.
—Gustavo Adolfo Bécquer (1836–1870), Spanish poet

O f the most spiritual and romantic places in the world, few can rival Florence, in the beautiful Italian countryside of Tuscany. The most recognizable structures in the Florence skyline are the octagonal dome of the Duomo (designed by Filippo Brunelleschi) and the Gothic Campanile di Giotto, the bell tower named after the painter and sculptor who designed it for the cathedral.

Whether you yearn for more depth in your spiritual life or more intimacy with your life partner, plan a lover's trip to Florence's Duomo. Go in September when the tourists have gone home and the Tuscan weather is wonderful. Get a walking map and explore this incredible city on foot. You can fly into Pisa, which has the nearest major airport, and then take the train to Florence's SMN railway station (under an hour), the bus, or rent a car. Florence also has a regional airport.

Soothe Your Spirit

Climb the narrow steps to the marble observation tower of the cupola to see spectacular views of the city, even on a gray day. Face your lover, and looking deeply into each other's eyes, offer a prayer of thanks for God's blessings.

A Deeper Look

The massive dome features a fresco, *The Last Judgment*, which took more than ten years to paint. Giorgio Vasari started the fresco, and Federico Zuccari finished it in 1579.

Basilica di Santa Maria del Fiore (Duomo), Florence, Italy

Basilica of Divine Mercy ◉

Lagiewniki District, Krakow, Poland

Jesus, I trust thee.
—Caption on the *Lord's Mercy* icon in Lagiewniki's sanctuary

After Sister Faustyna Kowalska, a Polish nun, passed away from tuberculosis, her relics were laid to rest beneath a painting of the image that had comforted and guided her throughout her spiritual life: her vision, in 1931, of the Merciful Christ. In the vision, the Lord instructed her to commission a painting of his likeness. In a later vision, Christ revealed His Dogma of Divine Mercy. The Merciful Christ painting was completed, and the sister's relics were entombed beneath it in 1940, following her death in 1938. Since then, the faithful have flocked to the shrine to pray or to give thanks for healing.

If you suffer from an ailment and seek spiritual support for a healing, consider visiting the Basilica of Divine Mercy.

Soothe Your Spirit

Visit the church for the daily special prayer during the 3:00 p.m. "Hour of Divine Mercy" (a reference to the time Jesus is believed to have died on the cross) and stay for the Chaplet of Divine Mercy. Or light a candle and pray before the icon for the healing you seek. The church is about 2 miles from Krakow's Old Town.

A Deeper Look

Consecrated in 2002 by Pope John Paul II, a native of Poland, the modern, monolithic Basilica of Divine Mercy receives two million visitors each year. The shrine with the Divine Mercy painting and the nun's relics is in the chapel of the old convent.

Basilica of the Dormition
(also Hagia Maria Sion Abbey)⊗
Mount Zion, Jerusalem

The quieter the mind, the more powerful, the worthier,
the deeper, the more telling and more perfect the prayer is.
—Meister Eckhart (1260–1328), German philosopher, theologian, and mystic

O n top of Mount Zion, just beyond Zion Gate, sits an organic-looking German Benedictine abbey with a blue conical roof punctuated with four turrets and a domed clock tower that safeguards the traditional site of the last "falling asleep" of the Blessed Virgin Mary when her soul was taken to heaven. The event is also known as the Assumption of Mary. Above the main altar, a gold Byzantine-style mosaic of the Madonna with Child shimmers with light and finds resonance in other sacred art that adorns the basilica.

If you are searching for spiritual meaning from sacred feminine images, are connecting with your higher self or soul in sleep, or want to see the traditional place of Mary's death (another tradition cites Ephesus), visit the Basilica of the Dormition. You can walk to the church from Mount Zion. Otherwise, take a taxi, rental car, or local buses. There is no admission fee.

Soothe Your Spirit
Study the beauty of the sacred art, noticing the imagery of Mary in the icons and mosaics. Pray in the nave. In the crypt a sculpture of the Holy Mother lays in repose, while in the dome above her, Christ receives her soul. Reflect on death as the final "falling asleep."

A Deeper Look
Architect Heinrich Renard used the cathedral of Aix-la-Chapelle as his model for the basilica. The Room of the Last Supper is located beside the abbey.

Basilica of Our Lady of the Rosary (Basilica at Fátima)◉

Fátima, Portugal

Mother is the name for God in the lips and hearts of little children.
—William Makepeace Thackeray (1811–1863), Indian-born English author

In 1982, Pope John Paul II gave thanks to the Virgin Mary for saving his life from an assassination attempt the previous year by embedding the bullet taken from his chest into the crown of Our Lady of Fátima. Built in 1928, the cream-colored neoclassical basilica stands on the site where, in 1917, three children saw six consecutive apparitions of the Virgin Mary, the third prophesying the death of a pope in 1981. The tombs of two of the children (Jacinta and Francisco) are housed in the basilica, and stained glass windows depict narrative scenes of the apparitions. At the center of this cathedral, which has fifteen altars honoring the mysteries of the Rosary, is the Chapel of Apparitions where a marble pillar marks the spot of the appearances.

If you wish to pray on behalf of your child or children everywhere, visit Our Lady of the Rosary, Fátima. Travel from Lisbon by rental car, bus, or by train and taxi.

Soothe Your Spirit
Pray the Rosary for peace or offer the simple prayer Mary gave to the three children at Fátima: "My God, I believe, I adore."

A Deeper Look
Four million people visit Fátima each year, with crowds swelling on May 13, the day of the first apparition, and on October 13, the day of the last appearance.

Basiliek van het Heilig Bloed
(Basilica of the Holy Blood)●
Bruges, Belgium

God is the strength of my heart, and my portion for ever.
—Bible, Psalm 73:26

Since 1149, this pretty little basilica has been the home to a fragment of cloth said to contain blood wiped from Jesus' crucified body by Joseph of Arimathea (who also donated his own tomb, or sepulcher, for Jesus' burial). The sacred relic resides in a glass vial adorned with a gold crown on each end, which is housed inside the silver side altar of the upper chapel. Many people speak of having a spine-tingling experience in the presence of this icon.

If your spirit needs recharging, come to Basilica of the Holy Blood. Located in the southwest corner of Castle Square, the chapel is accessible by walking, cycling, buses, and trams.

Soothe Your Spirit
Visit any day 11:30 a.m.–12:00 p.m. and 2:00–4:00 p.m., when the bishop of Bruges brings the relic out for public viewing, or on the Day of Ascension (forty days after Easter), when the bishop brings the vial out for a processional in the city. Let the relic work its magic on you and strengthen your spirit.

A Deeper Look
Presumably the relic was given to the count of Flanders by the patriarch of Jerusalem during the Second Crusade and was subsequently brought to the basilica in Bruges.

Basiliek van het Heilig Bloed (Basilica of the Holy Blood), Bruges, Belgium

Basilique du Sacré-Coeur de Montmartre (Basilica of the Sacred Heart)◖

Paris, France

If any man thirst, let him come unto me, and drink.
—Bible, John 7:37

The white travertine dome of the Basilica of the Sacred Heart shimmers in the light—and its panoramic views rival those of the Eiffel Tower. Few buildings in Paris can surpass the beauty of this Romano-Byzantine church rising regally from Montmartre, drawing admiring eyes throughout the city. The treasures inside are no less alluring; for example, the mosaic in the apse, *Christ in Glory*, is one of the largest mosaics in the world. However, it is the emphasis on devotion and prayer that beckons worshippers from near and far. Since 1885, the monstrance containing the Blessed Sacrament has been perpetually on display over the high altar. Parishioners and Catholic pilgrims come day and night to receive the succor of Christ's body (the consecrated host) and blood (consecrated wine).

If you yearn for deep communion with the Divine or for an answer to a prayer, visit the Basilica of the Sacred Heart in Paris. For an unforgettable experience, come during Holy Week (Easter) or Christmas. The nearest metro station is Abbesses, Line 12. No recording devices are allowed inside the church.

Soothe Your Spirit

Contemplate the symbolic meaning of the communion ritual. Pray for the insight or support you desire and then light a candle to perpetuate your prayer.

A Deeper Look

Montmartre was sacred to the Druids, the Gauls, the Romans, and early Christians (the Church of Saint Peter). The cornerstone of Sacré-Coeur was laid in 1875; the basilica was completed in 1881, but wars delayed its consecration until 1919.

Basilique Sainte-Marie-Madeleine
(Basilica Church of Saint Mary Magdalene)◗
Vézelay, France

I alone love the unseen in you. (Jesus talking to Mary Magdalene in Kahlil Gibran's Jesus, the Son of Man)
—Kahlil Gibran (1883–1931), Lebanese-born American artist, poet, and writer

When Saint Bernard of Clairvaux delivered his powerful sermon advocating the Second Crusade, he chose to speak at the Benedictine abbey now known as the Basilica Church of Saint Mary Magdalene. The Dominican church, a stunning example of French Burgundian Romanesque architecture, has been a favorite pilgrimage site since the Middle Ages.

If you want to show or be shown more compassion or to deepen your devotion to the Divine, visit the basilica to venerate Saint Mary Magdalene, whose name is often invoked by modern Christian women as an example of unconditional Divine love and unwavering devotion to Christ.

Soothe Your Spirit
Light a candle, and as you pray for the seeds of love and compassion to germinate and grow in your heart, feel the spirit of Mary Magdalene fill you with holy love.

A Deeper Look
The basilica's clerestory windows pierce the upper walls above the pews and are oriented so that at 12 p.m. on the summer solstice the sunlight enters through the panes and illuminates precise locations, suggesting that the effect was intentional. The nave of the church is one of the longest in France—a few yards less than Notre Dame Cathedral in Paris.

Baths of Aphrodite/Fountain of Love⬤
Paphos, Cyprus, Greece

Even if you gods, and all the goddesses too, should be looking on, yet would I be glad to sleep with the golden Aphrodite.
—Homer (800–700 B.C.), *The Iliad*, Greek epic poet

J ust north of Paphos is a site sacred to the ancient Greeks—the Baths of Aphrodite, where the Olympian goddess of love and sexual rapture bathed in a pool of a natural grotto under a fig tree. Today, the Aphrodite and Adonis walking trails along the Akamas Peninsula merge between the Baths of Aphrodite and Pyrgos tis Rigenas (Tower of the Queen), offering spectacular views.

If you desire to awaken or reawaken intimacy in your relationship, grab your partner and head for the Baths of Aphrodite. Winter, spring, and autumn are the best times to go, as Cyprus is hot in summer. No bathing is allowed in the pool, but there are great swimming beaches and coves just beyond the fountain. Fly into Paphos Airport and drive north along the coast about 29 miles, 2 miles past Latchi. Daily buses also link Paphos and Latchi.

Soothe Your Spirit
Walk the sacred lovers' trail hand in hand with your beloved. Sit on one of the benches overlooking the sea, wrapped in each other's arms, mindful to keep the passion of Aphrodite/Adonis alive in your relationship.

A Deeper Look
Adonis and Aphrodite's complicated love story is told in Ovid's *Metamorphoses*.

Bete Giyorgis Church of Lalibela⊕

Ethiopia, Africa

All loves should simply be stepping stones to the love of God.
—Plato (429–347 B.C.), Greek philosopher and mathematician

When Ethiopian king Lalibela envisioned building a New Jerusalem in the twelfth century, he created a complex of rock-hewn churches in Roha. The eleventh church, the incomparable Bete Giyorgis (Saint George's), was built as a beautiful memorial to him by his widow from a single slab 40 feet down and shaped into a Greek cross with a large access trench encircling it.

If you are in a spiritual slump or rut, shake things up with a visit to Lalibela. Visit this World Heritage site for Christmas or Timkat (the Orthodox celebration of Epiphany). Travel from Addis Ababa by air to Lalibela's airport. Or, take the bus (it's a two-day trip with a stopover). Outside the airport, take a minibus or horse-drawn cart.

Women are not allowed in the room where the saint/king's relics are kept, and only the priests are allowed in the inner sanctums of the churches where the rituals take place. Wear comfortable walking shoes with traction to avoid slipping in the passageways.

Soothe Your Spirit

Explore these Orthodox churches on your own or with a guide who can ask questions for you. Soak up the ambiance of this religiously oriented community with more than a thousand priests and unusual sanctuaries dating to the twelfth century, and you might just feel a shift in your spiritual perspective. Pray for deepening faith and transformation while at each church or at one that draws you more than the others.

A Deeper Look

To strengthen his power against his adversaries, King Lalibela may have built his monolithic churches in part to garner the support of the medieval Ethiopian Orthodox Church.

Bete Giyorgis Church of Lalibela, Ethiopia, Africa

Bighorn Medicine Wheel◐
Bighorn National Forest, Wyoming, United States

You have noticed that everything an Indian does is in a circle, and that is because the Power of the World always works in circles...
—Black Elk (1863–1950), Oglala Lakota Sioux medicine man

A n ancient Native American medicine wheel, 80 feet wide, lies in a desolate area in the Bighorn National Forest on the western peak of Medicine Mountain. Created by the Plains Indians but used by many Native American tribes, the wheel has a pile of stones at its center (cairn), from which spokes extend outward to a rim. Along the rim are six other cairns—possibly benches—that enable a person to face the center and see precisely the point on the horizon where the sun rises or sets during the solstice.

Whether you would like to learn about the medicine wheel's astronomy or tap into its sacred power, journey to Medicine Mountain in midsummer—the only time the site is accessible.

Soothe Your Spirit

Get an early start so you'll reach the medicine wheel before dawn. As the sun rises, declare what you desire and then pray for the forbearance and fortitude to make it so.

A Deeper Look

The Bighorn Medicine Wheel is part of an expansive sacred complex that has been used by various Native American tribes for more than seven thousand years. Prayer ribbons tied onto a fence are a visual reminder of their belief in the power of this sacred site.

Borobudur (Borobudur Park)✿
Java, Indonesia

Even death is not to be feared by one who has lived wisely.
—Siddhartha Gautama, the Buddha (563–483 B.C.), father of Buddhism

When viewed from above or a distance, Borobudur looks like a lavishly decorated, giant stone multilayer wedding cake whose round edges have been gently squared. This ancient (ca. A.D. 750) Buddhist temple is a nine-step pyramid carved out of a crag of volcanic basalt to form a three-dimensional mandala (diagram of the universe) topped by a Mahayana stupa (bell-shaped tower). Adorning the walls of the massive temple are 2 miles of carved reliefs (1,300 friezes) depicting the Buddha's journey from Samsara (birth/knowing) to Nirvana (rebirth/enlightenment). In Mahayana tradition, Nirvana is not a Divine end, or heaven, where eternal safekeeping/well-being is bestowed. Rather, safekeeping/well-being is achieved through the infinite/ circular journey of Oneness (sacred living).

Whether you would like to see an astonishing sacred structure or to take a step forward in your journey to inner peace, visit Borobudur on the Kedu Plain of eastern Java. Fly from Jakarta or Bali to Yogyakarta Airport; travel by rental car, coach tour, bus, or taxi to the park.

Soothe Your Spirit
Take a sunrise tour and watch the mist rise from the ruins along with the sun. As you circumambulate your way through the temple, release your fears and feel the peace of faith fill you.

A Deeper Look
No one knows when or why the temple was abandoned; most likely, it was due to the eruption of one of three surrounding volcanoes. In 1914, a British statesman discovered Borobudur covered in volcanic ash.

Bourges Cathedral●
Bourges, France

And he kneeled down, and cried with a loud voice, Lord, lay not this sin to
their charge. And when he had said this, he fell asleep [died].
—Bible, Acts 7:60

This glorious Roman Catholic cathedral with some of the finest medieval stained glass windows of any church in France rises above the fertile Loire Valley in all its medieval Gothic grandeur with a long nave and flying buttresses. This cathedral is dedicated to Christianity's first martyr Saint Stephen, stoned to death for blasphemy in A.D. 35.

If you would like to ask Saint Stephen to assist you in praying for forgiveness for an infraction or to lift your spirit closer to the Divine, then come to Bourges Cathedral, located at Place Étienne Dolet in Bourges. Bourges is about 156 miles from Paris by automobile; take the A10 and then the A71 highway. The nearest airport is Tours Val de Loire. Or, take the train from the Austerlitz station in Paris.

Soothe Your Spirit
Notice the beautiful stained glass windows (nearly two dozen dated to the thirteenth century) of saints. In this sanctified shelter, pray for what you want to release and to call into your heart.

A Deeper Look
Elaborately carved sculptures (one reveals scenes from the life of Stephen) cover sections of the west facade.

Brahma Temple✴
Pushkar, Rajasthan, India

The realm where eternal luster glows, in which the light divine is set—
place me, Purifier, in that deathless, imperishable world.
—Rig Veda, Book IX, Hymn 113:7

This sacred fourteenth-century temple dedicated to Lord Brahma, Hindu god of creation, rests on a raised platform at the edge of holy Pushkar Lake. Thousands of pilgrims from all over India descend on Pushkar each year in October and November. This is a holy time when the faithful ritually purify body and soul by immersing in the lake water before praying before Brahma and perhaps leaving a silver coin engraved with the names of loved ones who have been born or have passed away during the year.

Whether you have lost someone dear to you or you want to focus on creation (birth of a new project) and seek blessings, visit the Brahma Temple. The nearest airport is located in Jaipur, roughly 90 miles away and has regular service to Pushkar from major cities in India.

Soothe Your Spirit
Have a coin engraved with the name of your loved one or with your name or the name of your project. Leave the coin in the temple and expect Divine blessings to flow to you from the Hindu "Creator of the Universe."

A Deeper Look
The temple is constructed of marble, features a red spire and the image of a hamsa, or goose, and shelters a silver turtle that holds engraved coins. Inside, there is a life-sized image of Brahma and a small cave dedicated to Lord Shiva and marked by a silver door.

Buddha Tooth Relic Temple✳

Republic of Singapore

When the mind is pure, joy follows like a shadow that never leaves.
—Siddhartha Gautama, the Buddha (563–483 B.C.), father of Buddhism

Before the passing of his physical body, the Buddha mentioned in the Mahaparinirvana Sutra that viewing his relics was as good as visiting him while he was alive because the subtle energy of his relics upon cremation would become crystallized and remain ever serene without further tainting by nature. In the relic chamber of the Buddha Tooth Relic Temple, the Buddha's relics of blood, bone, intestine, brain, and tongue are enshrined and showcased.

If you believe your sense of safe passage through levels of spiritual evolution might improve from viewing the Buddha's relics and feeling the sacred subtle energy that surrounds them, visit the Buddha Tooth Relic Temple. The temple is located at 288 South Bridge Road in Singapore and is easily accessible with public transportation.

No photography, pets, or eating of meat is allowed on temple grounds. Dress appropriately; no bare skin should show, such as low-cut or backless tops or sleeveless blouses/dresses.

Soothe Your Spirit

Purchase incense or flowers in the Offering Shop after crossing the temple courtyard. Light a stick of incense or place flowers in the temple in front of the various Buddhas and bodhisattvas. Say a prayer with your offering and then visit the relic chamber.

A Deeper Look

The multistoried temple has many rooms and shrines, including a Buddhist cultural museum with many artifacts.

Byodo-In Temple⊜
Oahu, Hawaii, United States

The essence of love and compassion is understanding.
—Thich Nhat Hanh (1926–), exiled Vietnamese Buddhist monk,
scholar, poet, and peace activist

A stroll through the beautiful grounds of the Byodo-In Temple awakens the senses and inspires devotion. The lush tropical Japanese-style garden, the shimmering koi pond, and the 3-ton brass peace bell are all sacred accoutrements of the Buddhist temple that sits in the shadow of the vapor-enshrouded, jade colored mountains. Inside the timeless temple, the 9-foot Lotus Buddha reposes in sublime bliss, seemingly absorbed yet ever-present for the whispered prayers of the faithful.

Whether you seek an oasis of peace and love or just need to tune out the world for a while, the Lotus Buddha of Byodo-In awaits. There is a small fee to enter the temple grounds, but getting there from downtown Honolulu is easy by bus (an hour) or by rental car.

Remove your shoes before entering the temple and refrain from talking or taking flash pictures. For the best photos of the temple's exterior and garden, arrive in early morning when the sun is behind you.

Soothe Your Spirit
Light some incense, quiet your mind, and meditate on loving kindness, the practice of unconditional love for self, others, and the Divine.

A Deeper Look
Built in 1968 to honor Hawaii's first immigrant settlers, Byodo-In replicates a 950-year-old Buddhist temple in Kyoto, Japan. This nondenominational temple welcomes all people to worship, meditate, or simply enjoy the serene beauty of this sacred place.

Byodo-In Temple, Oahu, Hawaii, United States

Canterbury Cathedral●
Canterbury, Kent, England

I will lay thy stones with fair colours, and lay thy foundations
with sapphires. And I will make thy windows of agates...
—Bible, Isaiah 54:11–12

Canterbury Cathedral, the Anglican Gothic-style cathedral in England, has been a site of worship since its founding in A.D. 602 by Saint Augustine. In 1170, while praying in the cathedral, Thomas Becket, the archbishop of Canterbury, was murdered by knights loyal to King Henry II. Within three days, miracles began to take place; their stories are depicted in a series of stained glass windows in the Trinity Chapel. For centuries, pilgrims have meditated on these windows as they seek a miracle, pray, or repent.

If you feel sorry for some infraction and would like to offer your remorse to God, do so, and consider a pilgrimage to the church where the Holy Spirit is still felt and the windows still reflect light through Thomas Becket's story. Fly to Kent, or from London take the Southeastern Railway from London Pancras to Canterbury West Station. Walk the remaining short distance. Alternatively, drive the M2 or M20 motorway into Canterbury.

Soothe Your Spirit
Take time to feel the deep spiritual energy of countless pilgrims who undertook soulful travel to pray here. Express the sorrow held by your spirit and feel your burden lift.

A Deeper Look
The Trinity Chapel enshrines the martyred Saint Thomas's relics. Canterbury Cathedral is designated a World Heritage site.

Cathedral-Basilica of Saint Louis King of France◕

New Orleans, Louisiana, United States

Louisianan brave men, this bell whose name is Victoire was molten in glorious memory of this day of January 8, 1815.
—Inscription in French on the cathedral's bell

The Saint Louis Cathedral, the oldest cathedral in continuous use in America, was built over the remains of churches dating back to 1727. Located in the heart of New Orleans, the cathedral holds the crypts of notables of the city, members of the clergy, and the Capuchin Père Antoine, who spent his life laboring on behalf of the people of New Orleans. Wives, husbands, and children of early Louisiana colonists, settlers, and slaves were married, baptized, and mourned in the cathedral. Today, Masses may be requested, reserved, and said for a loved one. See the website at www.stlouiscathedral.org.

If you would like to see this New Orleans landmark and honor the families who pioneered and built the great city, visit the Saint Louis Cathedral at 615 Père Antoine Alley. Located near famous Bourbon Street within the French Quarter, and facing Jackson Square, the cathedral is easily accessible using public transportation or rental car.

Soothe Your Spirit

Attend a service in this lovely church with its gorgeous mosaics and other sacred art and let the holiness of the sanctuary speak directly to your spirit. Light a candle for the people of New Orleans.

A Deeper Look

When the cathedral collapsed around 1849 after a remodeling attempt, new construction began on the neo-Byzantine cathedral in 1907 using granite and marble as well as beautiful mosaics in the interior.

Cathedral Church of Saint Canice●

Kilkenny City, County Kilkenny, Ireland

The Lord is good, a strong hold in the day of trouble;
and he knoweth them that trust in him.
—Bible, Nahum 1:7

When Saint Columba and his fellow monks flailed in a storm at sea, the monks beseeched Columba to pray for their safety. He calmly replied that he would leave that to Saint Canice (who was eating his supper at the time on dry land). According to legend, Canice bolted upright, darted out of his house with one foot shoeless, and dashed into the church to pray for the brothers at sea, and soon the storm ended. Dedicated to Saint Canice, the medieval cathedral church in Kilkenny City is a Gothic jewel in the Close, a complex that includes a lovely old cemetery, a seventeenth-century cottage, a library, a round tower dating to A.D. 800 with 167 steps, and several other buildings.

If you long for safe passage, shelter from a storm, or protection of any kind, come to the Cathedral Church of Saint Canice in the lovely hill country of Ireland.

Soothe Your Spirit

While in the cathedral, ask Saint Canice to carry your prayer for your safety and security to God. Purchase a Saint Canice medal or locket to keep or wear to remind you of the power of prayer.

A Deeper Look

Saint Canice's Cathedral houses an important historical document that is relevant to the twentieth century: Ireland's Memorial Records, seven volumes filled with the names of the Irish soldiers who fell during the First Great European War of 1914–1918.

Cathedral Church of Saint Canice, Kilkenny City, County Kilkenny, Ireland

Cathedral of Christ the Light ∾
Oakland, California, United States

When two texts, or two assertions, or perhaps, two ideas are in contradiction, be ready to reconcile them rather than cancel one by the other...
—Marguerite Yourcenar (1903–1987), French author

The Christ the Light Cathedral replaced the Cathedral of Saint Francis de Sales in Oakland, destroyed in the 1989 Loma Prieta earthquake. The cathedral's ultramodern look is nothing short of astonishing—the wood, glass, and steel structure resembles a bishop's miter; the worship space is shaped like a vesica piscis (womb shape); and walls of wood louvers and glass flood the sanctuary with natural light.

If you want to find a place of hope and renewal to fill a void left by a devastating loss, visit the Cathedral of Christ the Light, located at 2121 Harrison Street and Grand Avenue, across from Lake Merritt. The nearest airport is Oakland International. To get to the cathedral, take Bay Area Rapid Transit (BART), as the Nineteenth Street station is six blocks from the church. If you drive, several nearby parking garages are available.

Soothe Your Spirit
Sit in the cathedral on a bright day to feel wrapped in a cocoon of loving, protective light while praying about your loss. Talk to a priest or spiritual adviser about relief, renewal, and regeneration.

A Deeper Look
The cathedral complex includes a public plaza and garden, the chancery offices including those of the Bishop's Curia, a conference center, a café and shop, a mausoleum with crypts, and a clinic.

Cathedral of Saint James ⬦
Innsbruck, Austria

Forsake me not, O Lord: O my God, be not far from me.
Make haste to help me, O Lord my salvation.
—Bible, Psalm 39:12–13

The Cathedral of Saint James (Dom zu St. Jakob) astonishes visitors with its ornate four-tiered facade, clock towers, dramatic domes, ceiling murals, high marble altars, lavish gilt, carved altar, and lavish embellishments throughout. However, one of the most outstanding treasures of this angelic eighteenth-century baroque masterpiece is an exquisite painting entitled *Maria Hilf* (Mary of Succor) by the German master Lucas Cranach the Elder on the main altar.

If you need aid or answers at this time in your life, visit the Cathedral of Saint James and view the icon. During the summer the cathedral opens from 10:30 a.m. to 7:30 p.m., except on Sundays and public holidays when it is open from 12:30 to 7:30 p.m. No tours or visits are allowed during services, and no photography is allowed inside the cathedral.

Soothe Your Spirit
Attend Mass and then sit quietly for a few moments gazing at the icon of Mary of Succor as you pray for the guidance or assistance you seek.

A Deeper Look
Built in 1717 to 1724, the cathedral's sumptuous interior was created by two Munich artisans, brothers Cosmas Damian (a painter) and Egid Quirin Asam (a sculptor).

Cathedral of the Madeleine◐
Salt Lake City, Utah, United States

Thou has turned for me my mourning into dancing:
thou has put off my sackcloth, and girded me with gladness.
—Bible, Psalm 30:11

The stunning Gothic interior of the Cathedral of the Madeleine is a visual feast: white-marble altar with gold veining situated on a three-step marble riser, scrubbed and shined hardwood floors, a plethora of exquisite stained glass windows, delicately carved wooden screens and pews, sweeping arches, and colorful embellished columns combine to create a breathtaking sacred interior. Through its sacred art, this Utah treasure reminds those who step inside that Jesus stood at the heart of Mary Magdalene's personal transformation story.

Whether you would like to venerate Saint Mary Magdalene or see the awe-inspiring cathedral under her patronage in Utah, take time to visit this sacred place honoring the woman Jesus trusted and loved, as he did all his disciples. The cathedral is located at 331 East South Temple in Salt Lake City, not far from Temple Square and the Mormon Tabernacle. There is an international airport and good metropolitan transportation, including buses and taxis.

Soothe Your Spirit
Make a silent confession and pray for forgiveness for a thought, word, or deed that you regret. Reflect on the special relationship that Mary Magdalene, who was not perfect, had with Jesus, some say as his closest friend, most loyal disciple, and trusted confidante.

A Deeper Look
The Cathedral of the Madeleine (the French spelling of Magdalene) was dedicated in 1909 and rededicated after renovations in 1993. It serves as the mother church for Roman Catholics in Utah.

Cathedral Rock☯

Sedona, Arizona, United States

A pile of rocks ceases to be a rock when somebody contemplates it with the idea of a cathedral in mind.
—Antoine de Saint-Exupéry (1900–1944), French author

This butte of towering red rock formations juts into the azure desert sky and stands upon one of the strongest energy vortexes on Earth, making it a favorite destination for New Age devotees. But the site has always been sacred to the Yavapai (Native Americans) who have occupied Sedona (*Wipik*) for centuries. According to legend, a couple who were deeply in love but arguing bitterly drew the attention of the Great Spirit, who chastised them for failing to appreciate the beauty of their union and the natural world around them. As a reminder to respect each other's views, he turned them into back-to-back pillars of stone—known as Lovers Knoll, a smaller formation between the two large spires of Cathedral Rock.

Whether your path of spirituality resonates with New Age beliefs or you would like to venerate the holiness of nature with a meditation on love, visit Cathedral Rock, 110 miles from Phoenix.

Soothe Your Spirit

Hike the steep trail to one of the saddles (viewing points) with your lover or a beloved friend. Meditate on opening your chakras (energy centers in your ethereal body) to receive Divine love and to transmit love back into the universe.

A Deeper Look

The energy of the vortex is thought to flow upward, which is believed to help connect with the Divine.

Cathedral Rock, Sedona, Arizona, United States

Cathédral Saint-Mammès de Langres⬤

Langres, Champagne-Ardenne, France

Children are the hands by which we take hold of heaven.
—Henry Ward Beecher (1813–1887), Protestant minister and author

The Cathédral Saint-Mammès de Langres, in the Champagne-Ardenne region of France, has twin towers that jut heavenward like outstretched arms beckoning angels to draw near to hear whispered prayers and to soothe the souls of families and children. Welcoming all who come to pray through its festive red doors, the cathedral is dedicated to Saint Mammès of Caesarea, a child whose parents were executed for being Christians. After his own teen martyrdom, Mammès's relics were taken to the cathedral in Langres in 1209 to be safeguarded along with those of martyred Cappadocian triplets, Saints Speusippus, Eleusippus, and Melapsippus.

If you are inspired by the faith of a child and wish to pray for children or for the souls of the child-saints whose relics are enshrined in the Cathédral Saint-Mammès de Langres, visit the cathedral, which is roughly an hour's drive northeast of Dijon or 183 miles from Paris and is easily accessible by car or bus.

Soothe Your Spirit

Hold love in your heart for children of all nations as you light a candle and pray to Holy Mother Mary that your faith be as strong as a child's love for his or her parents and for protection and love for all God's children.

A Deeper Look

Dedicated in 1196, the cathedral straddles two styles: Burgundy-Romanesque and Gothic. It is a national monument of France and the seat of the bishop of Langres.

Chaco Culture National Historical Park●
Chaco Canyon, New Mexico, United States

Life is not a continuum of pleasant choices but of inevitable problems that call for strength, determination, and hard work.
—Native American proverb

In Chaco Canyon in northwestern New Mexico stand the ruins of an Anasazi (Pueblo) cultural center that flourished from A.D. 850 to 1250. Although no one knows why the Anasazi left, all Southwest Indian tribes trace their ancestral roots to Chaco Canyon and consider it sacred. That the Chacoan people were able to build this highly advanced community and to thrive in this harsh environment for at least four hundred years is a testament to their fortitude.

To fortify your spirit, take a day trip from Farmington, New Mexico (the nearest city), to Chaco Canyon. Allow at least two hours to drive to and from this remote location and several hours to explore the vast ruins. Bring a picnic and water, and make sure to follow the advice given on the United States National Park Service website: www.nps.gov/chcu/planyourvisit.

Soothe Your Spirit

Drive or bike the 9-mile paved loop, taking time to explore the guided trails of the five major Chacoan sites. Listen to the whispers of the ancients carried on the wind, offering encouragement or perhaps a solution to your problem.

A Deeper Look

This sacred gathering place for the Anasazi included fifteen complexes (great houses)—some several stories high, with hundreds of apartments (rooms) and dozens of kivas (circular ceremonial structures)—designed for celestial alignment and built from quarried sandstone and timber hauled from up to 70 miles away.

Chapel of the Ascension✴

Jerusalem, Israel

And he led them out as far as to Bethany, and he lifted up his hands,
and blessed them. And it came to pass, while he blessed them,
he was parted from them, and carried up into heaven.
—Bible, Luke 24:50–51

A brick octagonal chapel with a dome marks the sacred site on the Mount of Olives where, according to tradition, Christ ascended into heaven forty days after the Resurrection. The chapel was built over the ruins of Byzantine and Crusader structures in a brick wall enclosure dotted with hooks that secure the tents of pilgrims who gather to commemorate the Ascension and safeguards an imprint of Jesus' foot in stone.

If you have been thinking about the "footprint" one human life leaves in the lives of others or want to contemplate the meaning of Jesus' human body ascending into heaven, start the process in this chapel. It lies east of the main road that runs along the top of the Mount of Olives in the suburb of al-Tur and is easily reachable from Jerusalem and the Mount of Olives by bus, taxi, or car (there is parking near the entrance).

Soothe Your Spirit

Light a candle next to the sacred foot imprint and read Mark 16:19 and Acts 1:9–12 from the New Testament. Reflect on the metaphorical "footprint" that Jesus left behind in the lives of those who remained and consider the idea of ascension of the soul, using the spiritual or religious discipline that most appeals to you.

A Deeper Look

The Ascension of Christ has been celebrated since the fourth century. The Chapel of the Ascension is both a Christian and Muslim holy site; in fact, the Islamic-style dome reflects that in the thirteenth century the shrine was a mosque.

Chapel of the Holy Cross✆

Sedona, Arizona, United States

That the church may come to life in the souls of men and be
a living reality—herein lies the whole message of this chapel.
—Marguerite Brunswig Staude (1899–1988), artist who designed
and bequeathed the Chapel of the Holy Cross

L ooking like a modern cross rising out of an ancient mesa, the Chapel of
the Holy Cross is stunning in its simple but brilliant design by Marguerite
Brunswig Staude, a student of master architect/designer Frank Lloyd Wright. A
massive wall of glass—superimposed with a pale rose-colored cross stretching
the full width of the chapel and thrusting 200 feet upward from the stone
foundation to the roof—affords spectacular views of God's creation for miles
around.

The chapel, built in 1956, sits on Coconino National Forest land near the
New Age mecca of Sedona, where many believe four energy vortexes exist,
including one at the site of the Chapel of the Holy Cross. Visit this unique Roman Catholic chapel, which welcomes people of all faiths to infuse their souls
with God's pure love.

Soothe Your Spirit

Let your prayer of love flow from your
heart and across the breathtaking
Verde Valley with its towering red
rock formations jutting into the azure
sky.

A Deeper Look

Staude chose the chapel's site in
part because of a red rock formation
visible to the east that looks like the
Madonna and Child surrounded by
rocks that are praying nuns to some
visitors and suggestive of the three
wise men to others.

Charminar Mosque✷
Hyderabad, Andhra Pradesh, India

And know the help of God comes through patience and comfortable circumstances with distress and that difficulty is accompanied by ease.
—Shaikh Abdul Qadir Gilani (A.D. 1077–1166), Muslim cleric

When Indian ruler Sultan Muhammad Quli Qutb Shah prayed to stop the misery and suffering of his people from the plague, he vowed that if his prayers were answered he would build a masjid on the site of his prayers. His jewel in India, Charminar (Mosque of the Four Minarets), stands as an elegant sixteenth-century testament to the veracity of the sultan's promise. The mosque's Cazia (Indo-Islamic medieval) architectural style features four towering minarets (160 feet high) topped with bulbous domes that are embellished with petal motifs that may symbolize the first four caliphs of Islam.

If you seek spiritual rejuvenation, worship at this lovely mosque in the Old City of Hyderabad, in South India. Rajiv Gandhi International Airport is about 13 miles from the city. Local buses, taxis, and rickshaws will get you there from virtually anywhere in Hyderabad.

Soothe Your Spirit
Pray in the mosque's open area during Friday prayers (with larger numbers of people, men and women pray in separate areas) or in one of the four upper galleries inside the carved minarets (each gallery accommodates forty-five prayer spaces).

A Deeper Look
The Charminar Mosque, built in 1591, has been called the "Arc de Triomphe" of the East. See it at its most spectacular at night when the mosque is illuminated.

Charminar Mosque, Hyderabad, Andhra Pradesh, India

Chartres Cathedral⬟
Chartres, France

And it was then that in the depths of sleep / Someone breathed to me:
"You alone can do it, / Come immediately."
—from "The Call" by Jules Supervielle (1884–1960),
French poet born in Uruguay, trans. Geoffrey Gardner

W hen French pilgrims could not travel to Jerusalem during the Middle Ages to do penance or to pray for forgiveness of their sins, they sought closer sanctuary in local places of worship such as Chartres, perhaps the most magnificent of the French Gothic cathedrals. With its flying buttresses, exquisite carvings, the two towers soaring over its pale green roof, and the effulgent light and vertical space in the nave, the church provided a beatific sanctuary for worshippers, especially those who venerated Mother Mary. The cathedral safeguards the Sancta Camisia, or cloak of the Blessed Virgin.

Whether your goal is to pay homage to the Mother of Christ and venerate the relic of the Sancta Camisia, which was given to the cathedral by Charles the Bald, or to spend time in self-introspection and prayer, Chartres Cathedral, about 50 miles from Paris, provides a stunning setting, on a grand scale, and spiritual tools (such as its labyrinth) for you to further those spiritual goals.

Soothe Your Spirit

Feel the vibe of the sanctuary as you enter the nave and notice light through the beautiful 176 stained glass windows that reflects on everything. Proceed to the 42-foot labyrinth; walk it with your mind and heart united in prayer.

A Deeper Look

The four-quadrant labyrinth was laid into the floor in the thirteenth century to help the spiritual seeker draw closer to God while following the labyrinth to its center. The walk ends on the rose, a sacred symbol in Judaism, Islam, and Christianity of the human heart unfolding to transcendent Truth that is God. If the goal was penance, medieval pilgrims would move along the labyrinth on their knees.

Church of Madonna del Ghisallo (Chapel of the Madonna of Ghisallo)◗

Magreglio, Como, Italy

Love conquers all.
—Encryption on dedication stone of the Museo del Ciclismo,
Pope Benedict XVI (1927–), elected to the Papacy in 2005

This tiny chapel on the summit of Madonna del Ghisallo—a steep hill in the Lombardy region of Northern Italy—is legendary among cyclists around the world. The legend originated in the seventeenth century after Count Ghisallo ran toward an apparition of Mother Mary as he was being attacked by highway robbers, saving his life. In gratitude, he built the church on the hill named for his Marian apparition, who became the local patroness of travelers. Later, cyclists adopted the icon as their patroness, and in 1949, Pope Pius XII decreed Madonna del Ghisallo the patron saint of cyclists. At the church's center is an "eternal flame" bestowing blessings on the thousands of cyclists—and other travelers—who happen by.

Whether you seek the courage to pursue your passion or the blessings of your trek through God's country, take a road trip to Madonna del Ghisallo. From Como or Bellagio, travel by rental car, local guide, or bicycle (fit, trained cyclists only).

Soothe Your Spirit

Pray for safe passage as you follow your bliss or continue your cycling adventure in Italy.

A Deeper Look

In 2000, when the building of the Museo del Ciclismo (next door) was approved, cyclists conducted a torch relay from the church to the Vatican. In 2006, Pope Benedict XVI laid the final stone.

Church of Our Lady

Bruges, Belgium

Listen to your life…Touch, taste, smell your way to the holy
and hidden heart of it because in the last analysis all
moments are sacred moments and life itself is grace.
—Frederick Beuchner (1926–), American writer and theologian

The art inside the Church of Our Lady in Bruges speaks to the soul. While Michelangelo's *Madonna and Child* beckons worshippers to remember the humanity of his subjects, the painting of the crucified Christ by van Dyck evokes the suffering of Jesus, and the tombs of Charles the Bold and his daughter who died at age twenty-five demonstrate that life can end in an instant and induce contemplation of life's moments as sacred.

If you want to discover your spiritual core or to see sacred art, visit this site. The church is located at Onze-Lieve-Vrouwekerkhof Zuid. Take the train from Brussels to Bruges (sixty minutes). The E40 connects Calais and Ostend to Bruges, as does the train. Various shuttle-bus services run to Bruges from Charleroi airport.

Soothe Your Spirit

Use your senses to see the potential for transformation or deepening faith in your life. Make this your prayer: "Holy One: Teach me to listen to my life. Bless my vision that I may see all moments of my life as sacred. Let me live in gratitude and appreciation for this blessed gift of grace."

A Deeper Look

Michelangelo created the *Madonna and Child* for the Cathedral of Siena, but when the cathedral couldn't pay for it, Bruges merchants Jan and Alexander Moscroen purchased it in 1506.

Church of Saint Anne✺

Jerusalem, Israel

*Now there is at Jerusalem by the sheep market a pool, which is
called in the Hebrew tongue Bethesda, having five porches.*
—Bible, John 5:2–9

When Saint Anne and her husband, Joachim, observed their beloved
daughter at play, most likely they needed to take only a few steps from
the house in which Anne was born and later their child, the Blessed Virgin Mary.
On the site, in 1130, the Crusaders constructed a Romanesque church featuring a domed basilica with a cross-vaulted ceiling supported by ornate columns
and capitals. Nearby, you can still see the biblical Bethesda pool, where sheep
were given purification baths before being sacrificed and where Jesus healed
a man from an illness.

Whether you wish to conceive a child or to venerate the patron saint of
childless and pregnant women, visit the Church of Saint Anne. The saint's feast
day is July 26 (July 25 on the Eastern Orthodox calendar). Reach the church
on foot or use local transportation, as it is situated near the Lion's Gate near
the Via Dolorosa.

Soothe Your Spirit

Breathe in the tranquility and pray
or give thanks for the blessing
of parenthood in this sanctuary
honoring the grandmother of Jesus
and mother of the Virgin Mary
(in Roman Catholic and Islamic
traditions) and the Forebear of God
(in Eastern Orthodox tradition).

A Deeper Look

In 1856, the Ottoman sultan,
appreciative of French support during
the Crimean War, subsequently
gifted the Church of Saint Anne to
the Roman Catholic White Fathers.

Church of the Holy Sepulchre✵
Jerusalem, Israel

And when the Sabbath was past, Mary Magdalene, and Mary the mother of James, and Salome, had bought sweet spices, that they might come and anoint him. And very early in the morning of the first day of the week, they came unto the sepulchre at the rising of the sun. And they said among themselves, Who shall roll us away the stone from the door of the sepulchre?
—Bible, Mark 16:1–3

Illuminated by candles and shimmering lamps, the golden sculpted images of Christ on the cross and his mother sparkle inside the Church of the Holy Sepulchre located in Jerusalem's walled Old City. Also known as the Church of the Resurrection by Orthodox Christians, it stands on the hallowed sites where Jesus was crucified and his body was taken for burial.

If you seek solace through a heartfelt connection to Christ's death and Resurrection, this site offers you a place for deep reflection and prayer. Step through the south transept's single door where a Roman-style facade with foliate moldings and pointed arches visually announce a holy place. Pause to consider the symbolism of the raised slab of stone where Jesus' body was readied for burial.

Soothe Your Spirit
Walk slowly through the church, tune into the spiritual energies of centuries of pilgrims. Light a candle and pray for a departed soul or for someone who is distant or in distress. If you cannot travel to Jerusalem, take a virtual tour: www.3disrael.com/jerusalem/Church_of_the_Holy_Sepulcher.cfm.

A Deeper Look
The Roman Catholic, Armenian Apostolic, and Greek Orthodox churches share this holy site and are responsible for its safekeeping.

Church of the Pater Noster✹
Jerusalem, Israel

Our Father, who art in heaven, hallowed be thy name...
forgive us our debts as we forgive our debtors.
—Bible, Matthew 6:9–12; Luke 11:1–4

U nder the ruins of a fourth-century A.D. basilica built by Roman emperor Constantine I, evidence of the holy cave long associated with the Ascension of Jesus was discovered in 1910. At that sacred location where Jesus taught his followers to pray the "Our Father" and to forgive those who trespassed against them, Constantine's Church of the Disciples basilica was constructed. The church was destroyed in A.D. 614, rebuilt in 1152, abandoned during the Crusades, and finally became the site of a nineteenth-century Carmelite Convent that moved nearby after evidence of the ancient cave was rediscovered.

If you would like to immerse yourself in the atmosphere of the holy site where the Lord taught his followers the most famous prayer in Christendom, visit the partially reconstructed Church of the Pater Noster and see the sacred prayer inscribed in many languages on colorful plaques lining the nearby convent walls.

Soothe Your Spirit

When you visit the cloister of the convent, chant the "Our Father" and meditate on forgiveness. Breathe in, breathe out, and let go. Don't probe the wound anymore.

A Deeper Look

The partially restored Byzantine church closely follows the fourth-century church's dimensions. When the church was rebuilt in 1152, the funds were provided by the bishop of Denmark who, according to tradition and legend, was subsequently buried there.

Church of the Primacy of Peter⊗

Tabgha, Galilee, Israel

So when they had dined, Jesus saith to Simon Peter, Simon, son of Jonas, lovest thou me more than these? He saith unto him, Yea, Lord; thou knowest that I love thee. He saith unto him, Feed my lambs.
—Bible, John 21:15

There have been several iterations of churches upon the holy site that commemorates the place where the resurrected Jesus gave Peter charge of his flock of followers. When Peter came ashore from fishing with other disciples, his nets were full, thanks to Jesus telling him to fish on the right side of the boat. Three times Jesus asked Peter whether he loved him, and Peter replied yes (in contrast to his previous three denials of Jesus, Luke 22:54–62).

If you have doubted your love for God or the Divine's love for you, reaffirm your love as Peter did, redeeming himself. Visit the Franciscan Church of the Primacy of Peter in Tabgha. To get to the site, take a taxi or bus from Tiberius. The church opens daily 8:00 a.m. to 12 p.m., and then from 2:00 to 5:00 p.m. Entrance is free.

Soothe Your Spirit

Pray for Divine love as sustenance to feed your soul.

A Deeper Look

The plain stone church is located at the edge of the northwestern corner of the Sea of Galilee and a part of its altar is a piece of the stone table (Mensa Christi) where Christ laid out the bread when appearing to his disciples after the Resurrection.

Convent of San Antonio de Padua (Saint Anthony of Padua) ●
Izamal, Yucatán, Mexico

He prays best who does not know he is praying.
—Saint Anthony of Padua (1195–1231), Portuguese Catholic priest

This convent and cathedral dedicated to Saint Anthony of Padua (Lisbon), revered for his fierce love of God, sits atop the ruins of Pap-Hol-Chac, a Mayan pyramid honoring Chac (god of rain). The convent's foundation is made of stones taken from the pyramid, toppled by conquistadores around 1549. The former monastery, built in a traditional fortress-like Franciscan style, features yellow stucco walls (replicated in many colonial buildings throughout town), sixteenth-century frescoes, and a statue of the Virgin of the Immaculate Conception, the patron saint of the Yucatán. A bronze statue of Pope John Paul II, who visited in 1993, keeps company in the courtyard with a Mayan sun stone.

If you believe Divine love can unite diverse ethnic and religious communities and would like to experience a place where that has manifested, visit Izamal. Located 42 miles east of Mérida, the capital of Yucatán, Izamal is accessible by bus or car.

Soothe Your Spirit
Attend Mass in the chapel or just contemplate as you stroll through the huge atrium (second only to Saint Peter's in Rome). Let the spiritual energy of this sanctuary ignite in your heart a fierce love of God.

A Deeper Look
Izamal was one of the oldest and most sacred Mayan cities. Today, the town is a harmonious blend of Mayan, colonial, and modern cultures and one of thirty-five *pueblos magicos* (magical villages) designated by Mexico's Ministry of Tourism.

Convent of San Antonio de Padua (Saint Anthony of Padua), Izamal, Yucatán, Mexico

Convento de Santa Teresa, Ávila (Convent of Saint Teresa of Ávila) ⌃
Ávila, Spain

Pain is never permanent.
—Saint Teresa of Ávila (1515–1582), Spanish-born mystic and Carmelite nun

When Teresa, daughter of a Spanish nobleman, prayed to Saint Joseph for a cure for the crippling illness that plagued her during childhood, she was healed. Perhaps this explains, in part, the young girl's fascination with saints (reading about them, pretending to be an aesthetic) as well as her decision to join a Carmelite convent as a teenager. She later reformed the convent into a stricter Discalced (shoeless) Carmelite convent.

If you desire Teresa's intercession to overcome illness, come to her convent. It's an easy day trip by train or bus from Madrid (68 miles). Erected in 1636 over the house in which Teresa was born, the convent is still an active religious facility. Certain areas are restricted, but you can enter the elaborately decorated chapel with a baroque altar and statue of the saint.

Soothe Your Spirit
Pray for Divine healing using the simple type of prayer Saint Teresa preferred: "Lord, hold me, love me, heal me." Tune into the subtle vibration that is said to permeate the convent and to which are attributed many miraculous healings.

A Deeper Look
A fragrance known to Catholics as the "odor of sanctity" filled Saint Teresa's monastic cell in Ávila on the night of her death (although she was traveling and not in the room when she died) and wafted from her coffin when it was exhumed 330 years after her death.

Coventry Cathedral ◉
Coventry, Midlands, England

You will know that forgiveness has begun when you recall those who hurt you and feel the power to wish them well.
—Lewis B. Smedes (1921–2002), American ethicist and theologian

The morning after the Luftwaffe bombed their cathedral on November 14, 1940, the people of Coventry, led by the vision of their spiritual leader Provost Richard Howard, decided to rebuild in the spirit of forgiveness and reconciliation. The new Coventry Cathedral, dedicated to Saint Michael, rises in glorious splendor next to the decimated ruins of the blitzed medieval cathedral, and linking them are two sacred works: the Cross of Nails, from nails found in the ruins, and *Reconciliation*, a beautiful bronze sculpture.

If you want to work on forgiveness and also learn more about reconciliation and peace, visit Coventry Cathedral, located in the West Midlands District of England at 1 Hill Top, Coventry. The nearest airport is in Birmingham and the nearest train station is in Coventry, a ten-minute walk to the cathedral. If you go by rental car, there is parking a short distance away. The cathedral is free to enter.

Soothe Your Spirit
Visit the new cathedral as well as the ruins of the medieval church next door and reflect upon the destruction as well as the new construction as departure points into your prayer for reconciliation and world peace.

A Deeper Look
Both the wooden cross, made of charred beams from the ruins, and the cross of nails, made from the nails found in the rubble, were created after the bombing and have become symbols for peace and reconciliation around the world.

Cozumel◐
Quintana Roo, Mexico

I'm aware of the mystery around us...coincidences,
premonitions, emotions, dreams, the power of nature, magic.
—Isabel Allende (1942–), Peruvian-born Chilean-American writer

When an ancient Maya woman wanted to become pregnant, she would appeal to Ix Chel, the moon goddess. From time immemorial, the effects of a full moon on sex and fertility have been observable: heightened romantic passion and increases in labor and childbirth. Since the entire island of Cozumel is the holy domain of the Mayan moon goddess, you might want to perform your own fertility ritual (perhaps with your lover) under a full moon on a romantic Cozumel beach.

Cozumel (Place of Swallows) is small: only 30 miles wide and not quite 10 miles across. Yet the island, which lies 37 miles south of Cancún, is one of Mexico's most popular tourist destinations because of its pristine beaches and incredible snorkeling on the Mesoamerican Reef.

Travel to Cozumel is easy now that the island has a small international airport with flights to and from mainland Mexico and many cities in the United States. Cruise ships also dock at one of three piers.

Soothe Your Spirit
As you sit under the stars sipping Mayan drinking chocolate spiced with chili and gazing at the moon, invoke the moon goddess's powers to bless you with motherhood as she has blessed Maya women for thousands of years.

A Deeper Look
The Maya believed the cacao tree was a gift from the gods and attributed eating and drinking chocolate to fertility.

Crater Lake National Park ◗

Oregon, United States

When one of the tribe felt called upon to become a teacher and healer,
he spent several weeks on the shore of the lake in fasting,
in communion with the dead, and in prayer.
—A.G. Walling (writing in 1884 about Crater Lake),
nineteenth-century American historian

When southern Oregon's volcanic Mount Mazama erupted 7,700 years ago, the mountain collapsed, creating a caldera that heavy precipitation would fill to form Crater Lake, at 1,943 feet the deepest lake completely in the United States. Located in a wilderness preserve protected by the National Park Service, Crater Lake has been a *gii-was* (most sacred place) to Native Americans for more than thirteen thousand years. Klamath, Modoc, Yahooskin, Cow Creek Umpquas, and other tribes traveled to the lake for vision quests. Many believed that swimming in the water or sleeping next to the lake with its volcanic Wizard Island would endow them with shamanic powers.

If you need to heal yourself in a peaceful and mystical natural sanctuary, visit Crater Lake—119 miles from Bend (north entrance) and 77 miles from Medford (west entrance). Though open year-round, the North Entrance Road and Rim Drive are closed mid-October through mid-June, when many trails and facilities are also closed due to heavy snowfall.

Soothe Your Spirit

Motor around the 33-mile Rim Drive, take a guided boat tour, or bike or walk along the lake. Feel the tension leave your body, mind, and spirit.

A Deeper Look

This most-sacred lake remained a secret of the Klamath Indians until it was discovered by gold prospectors in 1853.

Crater Lake National Park, Oregon, United States

Crypt of Yogananda☯
Glendale, California, United States

I give my love to all thirsty hearts, both to those
who love me and those who do not love me.
—Paramahansa Yogananda (1893–1952), enlightened
spiritual leader and founder of the Self-Realization Fellowship

Called the Incarnation of Divine Love by both his successor and his own guru Sri Yukteswar, the enlightened Kriya Yoga master Paramahansa Yogananda passed from death to eternal life and was interred in Forest Lawn Cemetery in the stately Great Mausoleum, Sanctuary of Golden Slumber. Some people mark special dates of the saint's life and passing through a personal pilgrimage to places associated with his life and his passing.

If you are a devotee, love this great teacher and support his work, or want to pay your respects, consider visiting the mausoleum at 1712 South Glendale Avenue. Hours are 8:00 a.m. to 6:00 p.m. daily, seven days a week.

Soothe Your Spirit
Ring the bell for entry into the mausoleum and inform the security guard you desire to visit Yogananda's crypt to pray. Find the marble entombment site with the plaque that reads, "Paramahansa Yogananda March 7, 1952," and offer your prayer. Enjoy the holy energy believed to emanate from there.

A Deeper Look
Modeled on Campo Santo in Genoa, Italy, the Great Mausoleum is the largest building at Forest Lawn. Access to the mausoleum is restricted, and security cameras monitor activity; however, in the public area, there is a stunning stained glass reproduction of Leonardo da Vinci's *The Last Supper*, and in another area, there is a labyrinth modeled on the one at Chartres Cathedral in France.

Dakshineswar Kali Temple✱
Dakshineswar, India

Install my statue in a beautiful temple on the banks of the Ganges River and arrange for my worship there. Then I shall manifest myself in the image and accept worship at that place.
—Maha Kali, as spoken in a dream to Rani Rashmoni (1793–1861), Indian philanthropist and founder of Dakshineswar Kali Temple

A fter taking charge of a temple dedicated to Maha Kali in 1856, the young Hindu priest Ramakrishna Paramahamsa became so absorbed with love for Mother Kali that he would plunge deeply into ecstatic devotion and lose consciousness. This happened so often that he was relieved of his priestly duties but continued to live in the temple complex. The three-story Kali Temple, with its nine spires, is built in traditional Bengali style and surrounded by an enormous courtyard housing other smaller temples. The temple seems to rise from the nearby sacred Ganges as if it were a lotus with petals (instead of turrets) turned upward toward heaven.

If you would like to see where Ramakrishna lived, absorbed in ecstatic love for Divine Mother, visit Dakshineswar Kali Temple—preferably during the dry season (September to May). During holidays such as Diwali in October or November, the complex is packed with pilgrims. Travel from Calcutta by rental car, taxi, or local bus or rail service.

Soothe Your Spirit
Purchase a red flower to offer inside the temple, since red is Kali's favorite color. Then pray for blessings of love from the Mother of Infinite Love.

A Deeper Look
In addition to the Kali temple, the compound features twelve shrines to Shiva (Kali's companion) and a temple venerating Lord Krishna.

Dhamek Stupa✹
Sarnath, Uttar Pradesh, India

Bring us, Powerful One, all blessings, all facility...
the best of treasures: the efficient mind and spiritual luster...
—Rig Veda, Book II, Hymn 21:6

After Buddha attained enlightenment, he received Divine inspiration to impart spiritual wisdom to his five disciples. At a deer park in Sarnath, roughly 8 miles from Varanasi, Buddha shared his Divine knowledge of the Middle Way. Today, Dhamek Stupa sits upon the holy site of Buddha's first sermon, looking like a giant red-brick cylinder with a collar of lighter stones encircling its base.

If you seek inner guidance or want to begin sharing your spiritual insights with others, visit this sacred pilgrimage site. The best months to go are August through March. The nearest airport is in Babatpur (18 miles from Sarnath), with daily service to major Indian cities. Trains from Varanasi also stop at Sarnath.

Soothe Your Spirit
Circumambulate Buddha's ancient stupa (bell-shaped tower), spinning the prayer wheels as you pass the entrance and allowing your mind to receive insights and inspiration. For Tibetan Buddhist practice, walk counterclockwise while chanting *"Om mani padme hum"* to open your mind to Divine inspiration.

A Deeper Look
Built by the Indian emperor Ashoka, Dhamek Stupa measures 143 feet tall and 92 feet in diameter. Just before his death, Buddha named Sarnath as one of four holy places, which accounts for all the monastery ruins in the area. Although the site is often filled with tourists and pilgrims, it still radiates serenity.

Dilwara Temples ✱
Mount Abu, Rajasthan, India

God, our Creator, has stored within our minds and personalities, great potential strength and ability. Prayer helps us tap and develop these powers.
—Abdul Kalam (1931–2015), eleventh president of India

The Dilwara Temples are a cluster of five white-marble, intricately carved temples sacred to the Jains, a religious sect in India whose principles embrace nonviolence, forgiveness, and self-effort as the path to self-realization and enlightenment. These astonishing temples sit in a complex among mango trees and wooded hills and are unique because each temple is dedicated to a different Jain saint and named for the village to which it belongs.

Whether you need to forgive yourself or another or accept forgiveness, visit the Dilwara complex. If you are a Jain, you are welcome to bathe and perform the ritual puja; otherwise, enjoy a guided tour. Mount Abu is located 4,000 feet above sea level and easily reached by bus, taxi, or train (the nearest station at Abu Road links the Golden Triangle of cities: Delhi-Jaipur-Agra).

Soothe Your Spirit
Soak up the sacred ambiance of the beautiful temples within the Dilwara complex while reflecting on forgiveness, even self-forgiveness, because it injures your spirit to hold onto psychological wounds, anger, and resentment.

A Deeper Look
The temples are located about 1 mile from Mount Abu and are a sacred pilgrimage site for Jains.

Dom St. Peter (Trier Cathedral)⬬
Trier, Rhineland-Palatinate, Germany

His divine power has given us everything we need for a godly life through
our knowledge of him who called us by his own glory and goodness.
—Bible, 2 Peter 1:3

According to legend, in the fourth century A.D., Constantine, the first Christian Roman emperor, accepted from his mother the sacred tunic Jesus wore during or just prior to his Crucifixion. Constantine installed the relic in his new church in Trier. Today, this red-brick Romanesque and Paleo-Christian-style church, rebuilt in the eleventh century, is a pilgrimage site for the veneration of the Holy Robe of Christ, safeguarded in its own chapel behind the high altar.

If you feel a resonance with the early Christians whose spiritual forbearance was perpetually tested and who drew strength from sacred artifacts associated with Jesus, come to Trier Cathedral. The nearest airport is in Luxembourg, 31 miles away; Trier is also accessible by sea and land. From the airport, train and bus service connects to Trier, or you can drive. Bonn, Aachen, Wiesbaden, and Cologne are within 100 miles of the city.

Soothe Your Spirit
Meditate on the power of unity, symbolized by the seamless tunic. Feel the weight lift off your shoulders as you imagine being filled with strength and fortitude.

A Deeper Look
Over the arched south door of this church dedicated to Saint Peter is a lovely Romanesque tympanum depicting Christ, Mary, and Peter.

Domkirche (Graz Cathedral)◓
Graz, Austria

But the fruit of the Spirit is love, joy, peace,
longsuffering, gentleness, goodness, faith.
—Bible, Galatians 5:22

G raz Cathedral sits on the site of a previous church dedicated to Saint Giles, a seventh-century A.D. Athenian noble whose reputation of sanctity has grown through the centuries with each new miracle attributed to his intercession. Located in the central Austrian city of Graz, known for its extravagant architectural styles dating to the fifteenth century, Domkirche features a magnificent baroque interior; the eighteenth-century high altar, constructed of beautiful marble, has a stunning altarpiece depicting the miracles of Saint Giles.

If you seek Divine intervention for a financial or fertility problem, visit Domkirche. Graz is located 124 miles southwest of Vienna in the Old Town District, the entirety of which is a World Heritage site. The address is Burggasse 3, Graz, Austria. To get to Graz from Vienna, take the Autobahn E59 south. The nearest airport is Graz Thalerhof, 11 miles southwest of the city. Graz is connected to other major cities in Austria by rail service. The easiest way to reach Domkirche within the city is to take a taxi to Burggasse 3.

Soothe Your Spirit
Inside the chapel, light a candle and dedicate your prayer to Saint Giles, asking for the fulfillment of your heart's dream of fertility or financial stability.

A Deeper Look
On September 1, Domkirche celebrates the feast day of Saint Giles, patron saint of people afflicted with mental and physical disabilities, sterility, and breast cancer.

Domkirche (Graz Cathedral), Graz, Austria

Duomo di San Martino
(Cathedral of Saint Martin)◕
Lucca, Italy

Gloria in excelsis Deo. ("Glory to God in the highest," from the Latin.)
—Bible, Luke 2:14

The Lucca Cathedral of Saint Martin houses a unique sacred treasure: the miraculous *Volto Santo* (Holy Face), a carved wooden crucifix purportedly carved by Nicodemus (who accompanied Joseph of Arimathea to ask Pilate for the body of Jesus); unable to carve the face, Nicodemus fell asleep and an angel finished the work. The richly decorated medieval cathedral in the heart of Lucca's old town also has a finger labyrinth, its grooves worn deep through centuries of tracings.

If the veneration of holy icons or relics deepens your devotion or you would like to work with your dreams for revelations, come to the Cathedral of Saint Martin, but plan on arriving for the Luminara, or candlelight procession, on September 13, honoring the carving of the *Volto Santo* (perhaps done by miraculous holy light and the hands of angels).

Soothe Your Spirit
Incubate a dream: eat lightly, take a bath before bed, and meditate with your head against the pillow, asking for spiritual elucidation or guidance in your dream, affirming that you will remember the dream upon awakening.

A Deeper Look
Hidden in a cave in the Holy Land for centuries, the *Volto Santo* was discovered by a bishop who had a revelatory dream. This carving displayed today is a thirteenth-century copy of the original that was splintered away by pilgrims desiring pieces of it.

Dura Europos ✻

Salhiyé, Syria

I circle around God; around the primordial tower...circling for thousands of years...and I still don't know: am I a falcon, a storm, or a great song?
—Ranier Maria Rilke (1875–1926), Austrian-German poet

In the sweltering desert of Syria where sandstorms have circled and whirled for time immemorial, an ancient city lay buried along the Euphrates River, hiding the world's oldest synagogue and house-church. In 1920, during the Arab Revolt following World War I, a soldier digging a trench unearthed brilliant tempera wall paintings of biblical figures (now in the National Museum of Damascus), which later archaeological excavations (1920s–1930s) identified as ruins of an ancient temple. Other sacred treasures found on the site include a synagogue roof and papyrus scriptures in Greek, Aramaic, Hebrew, and Latin. Numerous historical artifacts and structures have also been recovered.

If you are spiritually edified by early Judeo-Christian religious and cultural history, visit Dura Europos, bordering Iraq on Syria's eastern flank, near the village of Salhiyé. Book a coach tour or day trip from the town of Dayr az-Zawr, north of Dura Europos.

Soothe Your Spirit

As you explore the ruins, envision a deep spiritual connection with ancient Judaic or early Christian culture. Offer a prayer of hope or gratitude for God's guidance and grace.

A Deeper Look

Visit the National Museum of Damascus, perhaps before visiting Dura Europos, to learn about the spiritual, cultural, and historical significance of this ancient city.

Durham Cathedral◠
Durham, England

I pray thee, loving Jesus... Thou wouldst mercifully grant me to attain one day to Thee, the fountain of all wisdom and to appear forever before Thy face.
—Venerable Bede (A.D. 672–735), English scholar, teacher, and writer

Durham Cathedral, rising majestically from a hill in northeastern England overlooking the River Wear and ancient Durham, is a stunning example of Norman architecture. Although the cathedral, built in the middle of the tenth century, no longer holds the eighth-century illuminated *Lindisfarne Gospels* that combine Christian and Celtic themes, it does safeguard other treasures, including the tomb of medieval scholar Bede, author of *The Ecclesiastical History of the English People*, and the relics of Saint Cuthbert, the bishop of Lindisfarne, described by Bede as "afire with heavenly love, unassumingly patient, devoted to unceasing prayer and kindly to all who come to him for comfort."

If you feel a spiritual link to Saint Bede or Saint Cuthbert and would like to pray for guidance, visit Durham Cathedral. From London, reach Durham by plane, train, ferry, bus, or car (A1M motorway). No interior photography is permitted.

Soothe Your Spirit
Attend a traditional service or the special service for peace and justice. Pray for Saint Cuthbert's comfort, insight, and guidance.

A Deeper Look
Cuthbert was so revered for his spiritual succor to others that when he died in A.D. 687, the wandering monks of Lindisfarne carried his body with them until they reached Durham in 995, where they enshrined him in the White Church, which is the site of Durham Cathedral.

Ek Balam ☯

Valladolid, Yucatán, Mexico

...From above, House of Heaven, where star people and
ancestors gather, may their blessings come to us now...
—Mayan Prayer of the Seven Galactic Directions

The open mouth of a jaguar forms the entrance to the gigantic Acropolis pyramid at the ancient Mayan city of Ek Balam (Black Jaguar) deep in the Yucatán jungle. The ruins of this once flourishing city also include ceremonial temples, a massive tower, and the ruler's tomb.

If you believe each human has an animal spirit for guidance and protection or if you are inspired by the highly spiritual Maya, journey to Ek Balam, open 8:00 a.m. to 5:00 p.m. daily. From Valladolid, drive north to Ek Balam, hire a car and guide, or book a tour.

Ek Balam receives fewer visitors than similar Yucatán ruins, partly because of its remote location and lack of facilities. The excavation is also less complete than other sites—hence, less crowded and less developed—making it more peaceful and more authentic to the time of the Maya. The site has one restroom but no refreshments. However, in the nearby village of Ek Balam is a refreshing surprise: Dolcemente, a charming hotel and Italian restaurant serving homemade pasta and its own organic vegetables and honey.

Soothe Your Spirit

As you explore the ruins, breathe deeply and let the spirit of the jaguar fill you. Offer a red flower in gratitude.

A Deeper Look

To the Maya, the jaguar symbolized Divine protection, spiritual strength, and earthly connection to the Great Spirit.

El Santuario de Las Lajas (Sanctuary of Las Lajas)⊕

Ipiales, Nariño, Colombia

The soul is healed by being with children.
—Fyodor Mikhailovich Dostoevsky (1821–1881), Russian novelist

The neo-Gothic Las Lajas Cathedral on Colombia's border with Ecuador rises majestically from a deep, green gorge of the Guáitara River, and its walkway spans the river. This glorious sanctuary commemorates the appearance of the Blessed Virgin on a cliff face in 1750. According to legend, a bolt of lightning illuminated a painting of Our Lady, revealing it to a deaf-mute girl, Rosa, and her mother, María Mueses de Quiñones, local Amerindians who had taken shelter from the storm between two large *lajas* (sedimentary rocks). The painting of the Holy Mother and Holy Infant, located inside a cave high in the mountains, was reportedly unknown until Rosa spotted it. If you seek spiritual balm for an arid heart, weary spirit, or physical ailment, visit this sanctuary. Take a taxi to the cathedral from Ipiales, and on the return to the village share a taxi or catch a small bus (*colectivo*). Bring warm clothes, as the area can be cold.

Soothe Your Spirit

Light a candle, kneel, and ask for spiritual or physical healing from Our Lady of Las Lajas.

A Deeper Look

On a wall along the road between the village and the church are hundreds of plaques thanking the Virgin for miraculous healings. The cathedral is a holy site of pilgrimage, especially on September 21.

El Santuario de Las Lajas (Sanctuary of Las Lajas), Ipiales, Nariño, Colombia

Ellora Temple Caves ✪
Aurangabad, Maharashtra, India

Where love is, there God is also.
—Mohandas K. Gandhi (1869–1948), Indian political leader and father of India

B etween the sixth and tenth centuries A.D., Buddhist, Jain, and Hindu monks carved thirty-four sacred "caves" out of solid rock in west India's Charanandri Hills. Spectacular examples of Indian rock-cut architecture, these monasteries and temples are adorned with exquisite carvings, architectural details, sculptures, and paintings. The Buddhist caves (numbered 1–12) were created between A.D. 600 and 800, the Hindu caves (13–29) between 600 and 900, and the Jain caves (30–34) between 800 and 1000. This World Heritage site represents a time and place when worshippers from three great religions coexisted peacefully and collaboratively.

If you believe that love and religious tolerance can bridge the differences dividing people, visit the Ellora Caves. The nearest domestic airport is in Chikalthana, about 7.5 miles from Aurangabad, which is also accessible by state bus and train from India's major cities. From Aurangabad, travel the 19 miles to Ellora by car, local bus, or auto rickshaw.

Soothe Your Spirit
After exploring the caves with a guide, offer a prayer of universal love to heal the world or of Divine love to fill your heart.

A Deeper Look
Although all of the temple caves are magnificent, the pièce de résistance is Kailasanatha (16), a massive, multistoried temple carved out of a single rock depicting Mount Kailash, the Himalayan home of Shiva, Hindu god of both sacred celibacy and spousal love.

Futarasan Shrine✱
Nikkō, Tochigi Prefecture, Japan

A single, sincere prayer moves heaven.
—Shinto proverb

Futarasan, a Shinto shrine on the slopes of Mount Nantai (also Futarasan) north of Tokyo, rises like a shimmering ruby above the misty haze at the top of a deep gorge of the Daiya River. The shrine's vermilion-lacquered Shinkyō (Sacred Bridge) straddles the river in a graceful arch, affording safe passage to this peaceful eighth-century A.D. Buddhist sanctuary. The temple venerates the kami (Shinto deities) of Nikkō's three most sacred mountains: Mount Nantai (or Futarasan), Mount Nyoho, and Mount Taro.

If you yearn for a peaceful retreat from the turbulence in your life or for peace within on your path to enlightenment, visit Futarasan Shrine, which together with nearby Tôshôgû and Rinnô-ji form the Shrines and Temples of Nikkō, a World Heritage site. The best time·to visit is in April, cherry blossom season, or early October, when the leaves change color. The train trip from Tokyo is about ninety minutes; the walk from Nikkō Station to the Sacred Bridge takes about twenty minutes, or you can take the five-minute bus ride. Or you can walk 220 yards from Tôshôgû or a take a forty-minute walk or ten·minute bus ride from Nikkō Station.

Soothe Your Spirit
Meditate or pray for release from whatever obstructs or threatens your spiritual or inner peace.

A Deeper Look
The kami of Futarasan were the tutelary (protective) gods of the Tokugawa shogunate, and the shogunate's founder and first shogun, Tokugawa Ieyasu (1543–1616), rests in eternal peace in Futarasan Shrine.

Gandhi Mandapam✺
Kanyakumari, Tamil Nadu, India

Each one prays to God according to his own light.
—Mohandas K. Gandhi (1869–1948), Indian political leader and father of India

W hen a hole was cut into the pale pink and white ceiling of the Gandhi Mandapam shrine, some may have questioned why. All doubt disappeared on October 2, Gandhi's birthday, when every year the midday sunlight streams through the hole and falls precisely on the holy spot that had held his ashes (before they were distributed), thus symbolizing the emerging light of independence that Gandhi's selfless efforts helped manifest. As India metamorphosed from an outpost of the British Empire to a free nation, the Mahatma became the holy beacon of hope for worldwide nonviolence until, and ever since, his assassination in 1948.

If you desire to pay homage to the Mahatma (great soul) or to pray at the shrine that held his sacred ashes, visit the Gandhi Mandapam in Kanyakumari, at the tip of the Indian subcontinent. Reach the city by rail or air from other parts of India, and then use local buses and taxis to visit the shrine.

Soothe Your Spirit
Stand before the black four-sided column on which the ashes of Gandhi were kept to reflect on the Mahatma's life and ideals. Ask for spiritual succor and guidance for yourself, the ones you love, and your nation.

A Deeper Look
The Gandhi Mandapam shrine finds resonance in Orissan temples, with its columns, towers, elaborate sculptural treatments, pilaster decoration, capitals, and needlepoint spires.

Giant Hill⬣
Cerne Abbas, Dorset, England

It's easier to go down a hill than up it
but the view is much better at the top.
—Enoch Arnold Bennett (1867–1931), English novelist

Cerne Abbas in northwest Dorset has a chalkstone giant carved into a hill-ock, waving his club and exposing an astonishing erection. Although the landmark's date of origin remains a mystery (possibly the Middle Ages or even the Iron Age), the giant has long been associated with fertility. According to legend, women who wanted to conceive would camp out alone, and young couples would make love on the giant—most productively, within his enormous phallus. Today, women living in Cerne Abbas have more babies per capita than England's national average.

The best way to see the giant is from the air, across the valley, or from the east side parking area off the A352 highway. Walking on the giant is prohibited; as a National Trust ancient monument, he is fenced off from the public. Reach Cerne Abbas, between the towns of Sherbourne and Dorchester, by bus or car.

Soothe Your Spirit
Walk the Giant Hill Footpath, taking in views of the virile giant and the fertile English countryside. Make the act of loving a sacred sacrament (get a room first, perhaps in a lovely local B&B) and toast your fertility—in whatever manifestation you cherish or seek—with a cup of tea and a scone.

A Deeper Look
Some speculate that the giant represented the Greek god Hercules, who also held a club.

Gingee Fort ✤
Gingee, Villupuram District, Tamil Nadu, India

When restraint and courtesy are added to strength,
the latter becomes irresistible.
—Mohandas K. Gandhi (1869–1948), Indian political leader and father of India

The thirteenth-century Gingee Fort, once called the "Troy of the East" because of its impenetrability, is actually a citadel complex built by the Chola Dynasty to protect a palace and temples, a mosque, granary, treasury, marriage hall, entertainment hall, "ladies' court," gymnasium, funeral pyre area, and sacred pool. Today, the ruins of these once-grand buildings occupied by Vijayanagara kings and then by French and British colonists remain a memorial to the fortitude of those who lived and worshipped there.

If you are inspired by symbols of power, consider a visit to Gingee Fort, now a national monument. The nearest airport is in Chennai (the capital of Tamil Nadu). The train station is in Tindivanam; from there, take a taxi, scooter, motorcycle, car and driver, or bus.

Soothe Your Spirit
Take your time walking the almost 3-acre site that covers three hills, each with its own citadel (fortress). Ask God, who bestows power and grace, to fill you with the kind of strength that fortified the inhabitants of this special place, attracting kings, foreign governments, and the faithful alike.

A Deeper Look
Occupation of the fortress-like hills of Gingee (also known as Chenji or Jinji) dates back to the Jains in A.D. 600. According to local legend, Gingee Amman was one of seven virgin goddesses who guarded the village.

Glastonbury Abbey Ruins⬤
Glastonbury, Somerset, England

Yes, Love indeed is light from heaven; / A spark of that immortal fire with angels shared, by Allah given to lift from earth our low desire.
—Lord Byron (1788–1824), English poet

The spectacular ruins of this twelfth-century Norman monastery rest on a knoll in southern England that was considered sacred by pre-Christian pagan religions and that inspired medieval legends of Divine and romantic love. According to one legend, Joseph of Arimathea, a friend of the Holy Family, brought young Jesus to Somerset after Christ's Crucifixion and built a church on the site, where he also buried the Holy Grail. Another legend has it that King Arthur and Queen Guinevere are entombed there.

If your heart feels arid, visit Glastonbury ruins to inspire tender feelings of love. Open year-round, the site also features a museum, a large park, and a Saxon/Norman cemetery. The nearest airport is thirty minutes away in Bristol.

Soothe Your Spirit

Walk the ruins while contemplating the legends of romantic and Divine love associated with this ancient sacred site. As you breathe in the fragrance of roses, feel the cool wind on your face, and listen to the song of lovebirds in the trees; reconnect your senses to your heart.

A Deeper Look

Stones from what may have been the first Christian church in England (second century) form the base of the west end of the nave at Glastonbury Abbey (eleventh century). The abbey was once the second wealthiest monastery (after Westminster), before all of England's monastic churches succumbed to the Dissolution of the Monasteries enacted by King Henry VIII.

Glastonbury Abbey Ruins, Glastonbury, Somerset, England

Glastonbury Tor●

Glastonbury, Somerset, England

The only words that ever satisfied me as describing Nature are the terms used in fairy books, charm, spell, enchantment. They express the arbitrariness of the fact and its mystery.
—G.K. Chesterton (1874–1936), English essayist, novelist, and poet

Rising above the wispy fog like a delicate prayer veil that covers the face of the English market town that is its namesake, Glastonbury Tor soars 557.6 feet above Somerset and has been a holy site, perhaps since the Neolithic era, according to anthropologists. At the top are the ruins of two old churches of Saint Michael and a fifteenth-century tower so tall you can view three English counties—Somerset, Dorset, and Wiltshire.

Whether you are interested in self-discovery or want to feel the powerful transformational energies of Glastonbury Tor, visit England's smallest city and its environs, which include an abbey long associated with Arthurian legend, the relics of Saint Patrick who ended his days at the abbey, and Joseph of Arimathea, who purportedly took his nephew Jesus there on pilgrimage.

Soothe Your Spirit

Walk in silence along the steep path or follow the complex labyrinthine course to the summit of Glastonbury Tor. Sit and listen to your breathing as it slows. When you are completely calm, feel the subtle vibration of energy around the site and pray to the ancients for close attunement with the infinite and progress toward self-realization.

A Deeper Look

The discovery of two bodies in coffins dated to 1191, supposedly those of King Arthur and Queen Guinevere, has spurred the belief that the legendary court of King Arthur and the Knights of the Round Table may have been here, but the site is also associated with the religion of the Iron Age Celtic people.

Govind Devji Temple❋
Jaipur, Rajasthan, India

While God waits for his temple to be built of love, / men bring stones.
—Rabindranath Tagore (1861–1941), Indian writer and Nobel laureate

At night, the light illuminating the graceful symmetry of the Govind Devji Temple, dedicated to the eternal lover Lord Krishna (affectionately called Govind), lends an air of shimmering otherworldliness to the shrine. Ringed by the craggy Aravalli Mountains, the City Palace complex in which the temple and surrounding Jai Niwas Garden are situated was designed so the king could view the temple's sanctum from his private residence.

It is easy to get to Govind Devji Temple using local buses, taxis, or rickshaws. While the exterior is enchanting, inside the temple the fragrance of incense, thrum of Hindi chants, and voices lifted in sacred song will draw you inward, deepening your love for the Divine.

Soothe Your Spirit
Visit the temple at night, when the exterior facade is illuminated and awaiting devotees release a collective cry of exaltation as the doors open for evening worship. Open your heart to sacred love as you gaze upon the statue of Krishna when it is revealed for darshan (the beholding of a deity in image form) or during *aarti* (the ceremonial clockwise waving of sacred light, a ghee, or purified butter, lamp).

A Deeper Look
Located in the bustling metropolis of Jaipur—known as India's "Pink City" with nine districts symbolizing the sacred divisions of the universe—the Govind Devji Temple and Jai Niwas Garden are popular destinations for tourists and the thousands of devotees of Krishna who visit each year.

Grace Cathedral⬡
San Francisco, California, United States

A peaceful heart leads to a healthy body...
—Bible, Proverbs 14:30

This Episcopalian treasure atop San Francisco's Nob Hill heals the heart while calling it to worship with its heavenly artwork (including replicas of Ghiberti's famed *Gates of Paradise*), stained glass iconography (the most stunning: the Twenty-Third Psalm window), and choral concerts. But perhaps the major attraction for the millions who flock to the cathedral from around the world is the amazing indoor labyrinth modeled after the twelfth-century Chartres Cathedral in France and a newer outdoor labyrinth open twenty-four hours a day.

If you wish to experience the restorative and transformative powers of the labyrinth, go to this "house of prayer for all people," located at 1100 California Street. Parking is a major challenge, so unless you're familiar with the city, the easiest way to reach the site is by taxi or cable car (the nearest stop is two blocks away).

Soothe Your Spirit
Walk the labyrinth, focusing on your breath and meditating on what ails or troubles you. As you make your way to the center, release the disease (or dis-ease) within you (purgation). At the center, pause to receive the healing you seek (illumination). Feel the rejuvenation of your mind/body/spirit as you return to the beginning (union).

A Deeper Look
Grace Cathedral was built in 1964 on the site of the modest Grace Church, constructed during the Gold Rush. Among the cathedral's many artistic treasures is the Keith Haring AIDS Interfaith Chapel altarpiece.

Great Mosque of Kairouan⊕
Kairouan, Tunisia

Friendship is honey, but don't eat it all.
—Moroccan proverb

The Great Mosque of Kairouan, built around A.D. 670 and rebuilt around 863, is the fourth holiest site of Islam and the oldest in Africa. The fortress-like mosque is constructed of dressed stone bricks. The interior's marble columns, stone floor, pyramid-shaped chandeliers, tiled mihrab (a niche that indicates the direction of Mecca), and carved teak pulpit were created with ninth-century materials from Mesopotamia. Porticos created with recycled Roman and Byzantine pillars frame the marble slab courtyard. The north portico houses the oldest minaret in Maghreb, and the current minaret is a massive square-based tower with three stories of diminishing size.

Whether you wish to ask Allah for wisdom regarding an uneasy relationship or to see an ancient Islamic site where the muezzin continues to call the faithful to *adhān* (prayer), visit the Great Mosque of Kairouan, located in the city's historic district, Medina. The mosque is an easy day trip by car or bus from Monastir or Sousse, but a guided local or packaged coach tour is best. Caftans are available if you come improperly attired. Remove your shoes and perform the ritual ablution. Non-Muslims may look inside the prayer hall but may not enter.

Soothe Your Spirit
Pray for a healing or a blessing. Show your gratitude by leaving an offering of food for the poor.

A Deeper Look
Some Muslims believe that making seven pilgrimages to the Great Mosque at Kairouan is the equivalent of a hajj (annual pilgrimage) to Mecca.

Great Pyramid of Khufu⊕
Giza Plateau, Cairo, Egypt

...the God sleeping in the soul of each person is awakened by the power of the pyramid.
—Papyrus of Ani (1240s B.C.), Egyptian scribe

Rising almost 500 feet with a base covering 13 acres, the Great Pyramid of Khufu is the oldest, and only, survivor of the Seven Wonders of the Ancient World. Built around 2600 B.C., this pyramid was the largest human-made structure on Earth for forty-three centuries. A feat of engineering, construction, and astrological genius unknown for centuries, it is the only Egyptian pyramid with upper chambers and a passageway that descends 200 feet into bedrock and then ascends to a portal that aligns with the North Star once every 26,000 years. Innumerable mystical legends are associated with the Great Pyramid: such as, it was a temple for ancient Egyptian rituals, a prophetic monument, a giant sundial, and it was constructed by either extraterrestrials or an advanced race that mysteriously vanished.

If you seek personal or spiritual empowerment, make a pilgrimage to the Great Pyramid of Giza, 10 miles west of Cairo.

Soothe Your Spirit
Stand in the shadow of this ancient marvel and feel its monumental stability and powerful energy ground you and invigorate you.

A Deeper Look
The Great Pyramid of Khufu (Cheops in Greek) is at the north end of the Giza Plateau, on which also stands the rest of the Giza Necropolis—including the Pyramid of Khafre (Chephren, Cheops's son and successor), the Pyramid of Menkaure (Mykerinus, Chephren's son and successor), and the Sphinx.

Great Pyramid of Khufu, Giza Plateau, Cairo, Egypt

Grotto of Massabielle⬤
Lourdes, France

Let us draw near with a true heart in full assurance
of faith...our bodies washed with pure water.
—Bible, Hebrews 10:22

W hen fourteen-year-old Bernadette Soubirous had a vision in which the Virgin Mary instructed her to dig in the earth until a puddle of water was revealed and to drink from it, she did as she was told. Today, the Grotto of Massabielle (or "old rock"), in southwestern France, with its bathing pools of sacred water fed by the spring exposed by that puddle, is the focal point of a large complex that attracts more than six million people yearly, many ill and praying for a miracle.

If you desire healing or to venerate Mary, visit the grotto. The closest airport, at Tarbes, is 13 miles from Lourdes; Paris is roughly 500 miles north. Take a tour or go alone, but be prepared for crowds since this shrine is the most sacred of all the Marian pilgrimage sites in the world.

Soothe Your Spirit

Pray the Rosary in the Chapels of Mysteries inside the Basilica of the Rosary. Ask the Blessed Virgin to take your prayer of healing to the Lord on her heart before sliding into one of the seventeen pools of sacred water.

A Deeper Look

Stunning views of Lourdes—encompassing the Grotto of Massabielle, Basilica of the Rosary, and Basilica of the Immaculate Conception (built directly over the site of Bernadette's apparitions)—are afforded from the summit of Pic du Jer, rising 1,000 meters above Lourdes.

Ħal Saflieni Hypogeum⬢
Paola, Malta

First in my prayer, before all other deities / I call upon Gaia,
Primeval Prophetess... / the Greek great earth mother.
—Aeschylus (ca. 525–456 B.C.), Greek playwright

This prehistoric hypogeum is an underground labyrinth carved from limestone with egg-shaped burial chambers (symbolizing the Goddess's regenerative womb). Its builders decorated the walls of the first level with a red ochre wash and painted elaborate spirals on the ceiling of the second-level Oracle Room. But the heart of this sanctuary (and necropolis) is a trilithon (a structure consisting of two large vertical stones supporting a third stone set horizontally across the top) within a larger trilithon within a still larger trilithon—symbolizing progeneration.

Whether you feel drawn to the Mother Goddess or to sacred cave structures, visit Ħal Saflieni Hypogeum, a World Heritage site. From Malta International Airport, travel by bus, rental car, taxi, or motorbike. Order tickets (from the Archaeological Museum in Valletta, Malta) in advance; only eighty visitors are allowed in each day.

Soothe Your Spirit

After touring the hypogeum— pausing to issue a silent petition to Gaia in the Oracle Room—take off your shoes and embark on a barefoot walking meditation or meditate as you sit with your bare feet on the ground, absorbing the earth's regenerative energies. (Pressure points on the feet correspond to internal organs: reproductive, brain, heart.)

A Deeper Look

Ħal Saflieni Hypogeum, discovered in 1902, dates from 3600 to 2500 B.C. *The Sleeping Lady*, a famous 5-inch sculpture found inside the cavern and now housed in the museum in Valletta, depicts a reclining woman, perhaps incubating a child or a dream of conception.

Hill of Tara⬤
Naven, County Meath, Ireland

The Irish forgive their great men when they are safely buried.
—Irish proverb

Near Newgrange in County Meath lies an emerald-green, grassy hillock named the Hill of Tara. This ancient ritual site of coronation and seat of power for as many as 142 Celtic high kings is also the dwelling place for the gods and entrance to the otherworld. The ancient Celtic earthmovers created structures on Tara such as the Mound of the Hostages and the Stone of Destiny, a megalithic stone that would render a sound when struck by the true high king.

If your spiritual beliefs are enhanced or informed by seeing sacred places of the ancients and their spiritual constructions, visit the Hill of Tara. From Dublin, drive the M3, exit at Junction 7, and follow signs for Tara. Go early to avoid crowds and wear good walking shoes or boots with traction, as wet field grass is slippery.

Soothe Your Spirit

View the audiovisual presentation at the visitors center first so you'll understand what you are seeing, then walk around the site and let the four-thousand-year-old landscape work its magic on you. Use your imagination and feel the energy of ancient spirits.

A Deeper Look

Tara Hill, where archaeologists say human activity dates to the Neolithic period, provides spectacular views of a quarter of Ireland's coast and mainland.

Iglesia y Convento de Santo Domingo (Church and Convent of Santo Domingo)⊕
Lima, Peru

Since love grows within you, so beauty grows.
—Saint Augustine (A.D. 396–430), bishop of Hippo

The Church of Santo Domingo in Lima (the "City of Kings") with its white facade and black wrought iron fence is a stunning example of Spanish colonial architecture and dates to the late sixteenth century. This beautiful sanctuary enshrines a statue of the Virgin of the Rosary as well as two silver urns containing the relics of Saint Martin de Porres, the first black saint in the Americas, and Saint Rose, patron saint of Lima, venerated for her fervent love of the Holy Infant. After becoming a Dominican nun of the Third Order at age twenty, "Rosa" lived in a cottage in her parents' garden, where she said prayers and performed penance.

If you believe, as Saint Rose did, that working hard for God, for the poor, and for your loved ones is a path to spiritual development, come to the Church of Santo Domingo. From Jorge Chávez International Airport, you can easily get to the convent, located in Lima's city center, by taxi, automobile, or bus.

Soothe Your Spirit
Light a candle and vow that even as you work to support your family you will also do your inner spiritual work.

A Deeper Look
This old Dominican church, built roughly when Lima was established, has three naves, a large cupola, and Spanish-style patios (back gardens).

Iglesia y Convento de Santo Domingo
(Church and Convent of Santo Domingo), Lima, Peru

Il Gesù●

Rome, Italy

Him that overcometh will I make a pillar in the temple of my God...
—Bible, Revelation 3:12

A fter Saint Ignatius of Loyola founded the Society of Jesus (the Jesuits) in 1540 (as the Reformation revolt was raging in Europe), the pope gave Ignatius a small church, Santa Maria della Strada (Our Lady of the Wayside). Although Ignatius accepted the church, he believed it was too small for the Jesuits' headquarters. Today on the site of the smaller church stands the magnificent Il Gesù (Church of the Holy Name of Jesus) whose exquisite sacred art includes a fresco symbolizing a spiritual passage that is the pillared gateway to eternal life.

If you believe that time on Earth spent in spiritual endeavor provides safe passage into eternal life or you would like to see the chapel enshrining Ignatius's tomb, come to Il Gesù. The church is at Via degli Astalli, 16, in the Piazza del Gesù (central Rome).

Soothe Your Spirit

Light a candle and pray before Saint Ignatius's chapel-tomb, the first on the left aisle. Pray for spiritual advancement and safety as you progress in this life, and thereafter.

A Deeper Look

Michelangelo offered to design the church gratis, but Cardinal Alessandro Farnese, the grandson of Pope Paul III, funded the project, and architect Giacomo Barozzi da Vignola drew the design.

Ise Jingu ✹
Ise, Mie Prefecture, Japan

Be charitable to all beings, love is the representative of God.
—Ko-ji-ki, Hachiman Kasuga, Shinto tradition, ca. A.D. 500

Ise Jingu, built in the third century B.C., is the most sacred shrine in the Mie Prefecture, Japan's area of sacred Shinto shrines. In ancient times, only the emperor, the empress, and the crown prince were allowed to step into "heaven" or the inner shrine, Naiku, dedicated to the worship of Amaterasu Omikami, Shinto goddess of the sun and spiritual ancestress of the Japanese royal family. Here, the emperor would pray for the protection and safety of his people. In medieval times, however, the samurai visited, and since the 1600s, ordinary citizens have worshipped there.

If you seek spiritual safeguarding, undertake a pilgrimage to venerate Amaterasu. Take the train from Nagoya, Kyoto, or Osaka. Or, catch the bus at Uji-Yamada Station; it takes fifteen minutes to reach Naiku. By car, take the Ise Expressway and exit at the Ise-Nishi exit.

Soothe Your Spirit

Adopt an attitude of reverence as you step onto the Uji Bridge to cross the Isuzu River; the river is sacred. When you reach the water ablution station, wash your hands and mouth. Then wash your hands again in the river before passing through the forest and ascending the stone steps to the main shrine to pray for Divine protection and good fortune. Taking pictures is forbidden.

A Deeper Look

The outer shrine, Geku, safeguards the sanctuary of the goddess of the harvest.

Kamakhya Temple✳

Guwahati, Assam, India

Tantra loves and loves unconditionally.
It never says no to anything whatsoever...
—Osho, or Bhagwan Shree Rajneesh (1931–1990), Indian mystic and spiritual leader

According to myth, when the womb of Sati (the Hindu Mother Goddess) fell to Earth as the result of a chain of events stemming from her father's disapproval of her husband, a large cleft occurred in the bedrock. On that holy site, a temple was built to venerate the goddess, thereafter known as Kamakhya (One Worshipped by the God of Love). The eye-catching temple—with seven oval spires, three golden pitchers, and inner walls covered with carvings of Hindu deity—is among the most sacred to practitioners of Shakti Tantra.

If you wish to meditate on a family conflict or learn more about tantrism, visit Kamakhya Temple, which welcomes people of all beliefs. Located 5 miles from the railway station in the Kamrup District of Guwahati, the temple is open from 5:30 a.m. until 10:00 p.m.

Soothe Your Spirit

Place your fingertips on the yoni (cleft in the bedrock, representing the origin of life in Tantra) and say your prayer. Outside, light a ghee lamp or incense and walk around the temple clockwise.

A Deeper Look

Built in the sixteenth century and rebuilt in the seventeenth century, Kamakhya Temple sits high on a hill looking every bit the medieval Hindu temple it is. Its sanctum sanctorum, located in a cave, is one of the most venerated Shakti shrines in India.

La Recoleta Cemetery⊕
Buenos Aires, Argentina

You leave old habits behind by starting out with the thought,
"I release the need for this in my life."
—Wayne Dyer (1940–2015), motivational speaker and author

La Recoleta Cemetery, built by the Order of the Recoletos in 1822 on donated land, encompasses 6 hectares in a highly desirable Buenos Aires neighborhood of mansions and estates enclosed by expansive gardens (many gardens were built in the late 1800s as a barrier against the raging yellow fever epidemic). Neoclassical doors and high Greek columns mark the entrance to the necropolis of crypts, mausoleums, statues, and graves with astonishing sculptures, many unique and beautiful motifs and artistic elements, and architectural styles including the art deco crypt of the family of Eva Perón, also known as Evita, in the center of La Recoleta (perhaps the lovely art accounts for comparisons between La Recoleta and Père Lachaise in France).

If you are ready to embrace a loss that you choose—for example, to release a bad habit, a relationship, a dead-end job, a negative pattern of behavior, or something else that may be holding back your spiritual progress—consider visiting La Recoleta as a destination for release.

Soothe Your Spirit
Stroll the grounds of La Recoleta, mentally burying whatever limits your spiritual progress and then imagine replacing the loss with something new. For example, start forming a positive new habit to replace a bad one that you release. Give yourself about three weeks to ensure the new habit has formed.

A Deeper Look
La Recoleta is a necropolis of the elite and safeguards the tombs of several Argentine presidents, governors, soldiers, writers, diplomats, the grandchild of Napoleon Bonaparte, a Nobel laureate in chemistry, musicians, composers, and writers.

La Recoleta Cemetery, Buenos Aires, Argentina

La Sagrada Família (also Basílica y Templo Expiatorio de la Sagrada Família)◗

Barcelona, Catalonia, Spain

A cathedral open for every buddy [sic], a place of spirituality with the Christian message, a place of fraternity for all.
—Antoni Gaudí (1852–1926), Catalan architect and designer of La Sagrada Família

La Sagrada Família (Church of the Holy Family) is an exuberant architectural allegory to Christianity that fuses Gothic, baroque, and modernism styles and makes dramatic use of religious symbolism. It is also gargantuan—with more to come. Although under construction almost continuously since 1882, the structure is expected to reach completion by 2026. Then, architect Antoni Gaudí's "masterpiece" will have three grand facades—Nativity (completed in 1930), Passion (building finished in 1976, completed in 2018), and Glory (begun in 2002)—and eighteen spires (eight completed) in ascending heights: twelve Apostles, four Evangelists, the Virgin Mary, and Jesus Christ (the tallest spire at 560 feet).

Meanwhile, worshippers and visitors continue to throng to Basílica y Templo Expiatorio de la Sagrada Família. The church's crypt is among the "Works by Antoni Gaudí" designated a World Heritage site in 1984.

Whether you wish to attend Mass, to pray for loved ones, or to see Gaudí's "Cathedral of the Third Millennium," plan a journey to La Sagrada Família. Travel from Barcelona—El Prat Airport or within the city by rental car, taxi, sightseeing coach, or public transportation.

Soothe Your Spirit

Tour the church with your family or a group of friends. Say a grateful prayer before whatever image calls you.

A Deeper Look

The consecration mass in 2010 was attended by 6,500 faithful inside and fifty thousand outside, with one hundred bishops and three hundred priests serving the Eucharist.

Lake Baikal (Ozero Baykal)✺
Irkutsk, Siberia, Russia

One cannot reflect in streaming water.
Only those who know internal peace can give it to others.
—Lao Tzu (600–531 B.C.), Chinese philosopher and father of Taoism

L ake Baikal, in southeastern Siberia, is twenty-five million years old, 1.2 miles deep, 400 miles long, and 500 miles wide, making it the world's oldest, deepest, and second-largest natural lake. This World Heritage site is sacred to local Buddhists as well as to the Buryat people, the region's largest indigenous group, who leave monthly offerings at shrines around the lake and on the lake's islands.

If you are on a quest to restore or invigorate your sense of well-being, Lake Baikal offers many options. Book a packaged or customized tour (some even include shaman purification rituals and ancestor spirit rites), or explore the region by boat, horseback, or trekking. From Saint Petersburg, take a direct flight to Irkutsk, known as the "Paris of Siberia," which is the nearest town.

Soothe Your Spirit
Leave prayers for holistic well-being or of gratitude for good health at the sacred inlets, islands, and monuments of this enormous freshwater lake, also known as the North Sea in historical Chinese texts.

A Deeper Look
The most sacred area of Lake Baikal is Olkhon, an island 8 miles from the northern shore. A cave on the island is thought to be the earthly home of Burkhan, the supreme deity of the Buryats.

Lake Orta⬤

Orta San Giulio, Piedmont, Italy

Orta, the Lord's watercolour, seems painted on silk, with the Sacro Monte towering above it...and facing it, the Isle of San Giulio, resembling Dante's airy purgatory, hesitant between water and the heavens.
—Piero Chiara (1913–1986), Italian writer

Nestled between the Alps in Northern Italy, Lago d'Orta is the smallest but most peaceful and romantic of the region's glacial lakes, and Isola di San Giulio is the most beautiful and sacred of the region's islands. The magnificent Basilica di San Giulio rises from the center of the island. At the lake's edge is the picturesque town of Orta San Giulio, home to Santa Maria Assunta Church, consecrating the end of the plague in the fifteenth century, and Sacro Monte (Sacred Hills) d'Orta, featuring twenty chapels with life-sized statues and frescoes devoted to Saint Francis of Assisi.

This enchanting place offers a serenely beautiful setting for a Catholic wedding or a spiritual retreat. From Milan, travel by rental car, taxi, or shuttle to Orta San Giulio.

Soothe Your Spirit

Take a ferry or water taxi to Isola di San Giulio and reflect on Divine love in the hilltop sanctuary housing the glass coffin of Saint Julius.

A Deeper Look

In the fourth century A.D., brothers Giulio and Giuliano erected ninety-nine chapels in the region. After driving an evil serpent off the island using only the sign of the cross, Giulio (patron saint of Novara) built his hundredth and last church on the site where the tenth-century Basilica di San Giulio stands today.

Lakshmi Narayan Temple (Birla Temple)✱
New Delhi, India

In prayer it is better to have a heart
without words than words without a heart.
—Mohandas K. Gandhi (1869–1948), Indian political leader and father of India

I n 1938 when the Birla family, wealthy Indian industrialists, decided to honor Vishnu (Narayan, the Preserver, when in the company of his goddess/consort Lakshmi, goddess of wealth), the family chose the site of an older temple on which to build. The Nagara-style Lakshmi Narayan Temple—with its generous use of polished marble and red sandstone, tall curved towers, lavish ornamentation, and exquisite shrines housing *murtis* (statues) of the deities—has been called an oasis of spiritual calm in an otherwise bustling city.

If you are experiencing uncertainty or scarcity in your life, pay your respects at the Lakshmi Narayan Temple. The temple is located near Connaught Place, an important thoroughfare in central Delhi, and is easily reached by taxi, three-wheel cycles, and buses. You will be required to remove your shoes and cover your bare arms, legs, and cleavage before entering the temple, and no cameras are allowed inside. Free lockers (with keys) are available for storing your camera, shoes, and other personal items.

Soothe Your Spirit
At the altar, offer a flower, and with folded hands, petition the Divine from the deepest recesses of your heart.

A Deeper Look
The temple was inaugurated by Mahatma Gandhi, "the father of India," with the stipulation that all people would be welcome to worship there.

Lateran Baptistery ⬣
Rome, Italy

That which is born of the flesh is flesh;
and that which is born of the Spirit is spirit.
—Bible, John 3:6

Long before baptismal fonts became an integral part of every Christian church, Constantine the Great, the Roman emperor who converted to Christianity, built a baptistery over a first-century villa and a second-century bathhouse in A.D. 315 and dedicated it to Saint John the Baptist. The baptistery's exterior brick walls date to Constantine's time; however, popes of the fifth and seventh centuries remodeled, restored, and added chapels and a large entry to this building that holds a green basalt font depicting the baptisms of Christ and Constantine.

If you are considering a baptism or reconciliation and a rebaptism, spend an afternoon at the Lateran Baptistery where countless Christians have been baptized since the fourth century. Located at the heart of the Piazza di San Giovanni in Laterano, the baptistery is easily accessible by taking the Metro C Line to the San Giovani station. Alternatively, take a taxi or bus from other areas of Rome.

Soothe Your Spirit

Feel the magic energy of the ancient holy place where faith moved thousands to take the step of baptism. Then visit the baptistery adjacent to the Cathedral of Saint John Lateran to examine your heart, recite a psalm or prayer, and infuse your spirit with hope and certainty.

A Deeper Look

At the baptistery, there is a chapel dedicated to the Christian martyr Cyprian, a magician from Antioch who used spells to win the heart of a pious Christian girl, Justina. He repented and was baptized; they married and, later, were martyred.

Le Mont-St-Michel (Mont-Saint-Michel)◔
Normandy, France

God is absence; God is the solitude of man.
—Jean-Paul Sartre (1905–1980), French existentialist
philosopher, writer, and Nobel laureate

Mont-Saint-Michel, a granite islet rising 260 feet above the Bay of Mont-St-Michel and separated from the mainland by a channel of turbulent water, is virtually impenetrable, and during the sixth and seventh centuries A.D., it served as a Romano-Breton stronghold. Yet, the site has stood as a sacred sanctuary for more than a century, since the first monastery was built there in the eighth century. Today, the Romanesque abbey and church built in the eleventh century to replace the Gothic monastery provides a place of refuge and safety for both the community of monks and nuns of the Monastic Fraternities of Jerusalem who live and worship there and the pilgrims who journey there.

Whether you seek respite from turbulence in your life or are fascinated with French pilgrimage destinations, come to Mont-Saint-Michel, a World Heritage site. From Paris, take the TGV to Rennes; then catch the regional bus. The nearest rail station is in Pontorson. Alternatively, you can rent a car or take a coach tour from Avranches or Saint-Malo.

Be prepared for the steep stairway to the abbey—the only access. The best time to visit is winter when there are fewer tourists.

Soothe Your Spirit
Soak in the serenity and sense of security emanating from these sacred walls. Pray for the release of trouble or protection from turbulence.

A Deeper Look
Visit the adjoining cloisters, where hermitic monks live in secluded devotion, reading scripture, praying, meditating, and tending their gardens.

Le Mont-St-Michel (Mont-Saint-Michel), Normandy, France

Leshan Buddha✪
Sichuan Provence, Leshan, China

When the river is deepest, it makes least noise.
—Proverb

When Chinese Buddhist monk Hai Tong wanted to still the treacherous, turbulent waters near Leshan (an extremely holy area of Sichuan Provence) at the convergence of three rivers, which were the bane of local fishermen and their vessels, he decided to build a giant statue of Buddha into the cliffs. He started the project in A.D. 713, and his disciples finished it in 803. Because of the massive amounts of earth and stone removed, the course of the confluence shifted, the waters became calmer, and fishermen felt safer.

If feelings of safety are important for your spiritual life, come and see the Leshan Buddha. The Buddha is lodged against Mount Emei. Fly to Chengdu Shuangliu International Airport and drive to Leshan (about 93 miles). The cities of Emei and Leshan are also connected by freeway, train, and bus, and there is ferry service to Mount Emei Park.

Soothe Your Spirit

Take a ferry to approach the Buddha by water. Try to imagine how turbulent the river must have been in the eighth century before the construction of the giant Buddha calmed the turbulence. Allow feelings of safety and security to arise and offer thanks to the Buddha and his servant Hai Tong.

A Deeper Look

The Leshan Buddha is the world's tallest stone-carved seated Buddha and is a World Heritage site.

Lichfield Cathedral◖

Lichfield, Staffordshire, England

Sometimes the Lord rides out the storm with us and other times He calms the restless sea around us. Most of all, He calms the storm inside us in our deepest inner soul.
—Lloyd John Ogilvie (1930–), American Presbyterian minister and former chaplain of the United States Senate (1995–2003)

Lichfield Cathedral with its Flemish stained glass windows, octagonal Chapter House, beautiful Lady Chapel, and three spires affectionately called "the Ladies of the Vale" dominates Lichfield's architecture, even though it is one of England's smallest cathedrals. This tiny hamlet in the English Midlands has been a center of worship and religious teaching since A.D. 669. So, it's not surprising that one of its most impressive buildings, Lichfield Cathedral, safeguards numerous sacred treasures: among them, the *Lichfield Gospels*, an eighth-century illuminated manuscript; a fifteenth-century mural of the Crucifixion; and the shrine of Saint Chad, the seventh-century bishop of Mercia.

If your heart yearns for spiritual knowledge and you find medieval religious art fascinating, visit Lichfield Cathedral. Travel from Birmingham (17 miles south) or London (124 miles southeast) to Lichfield by bus, taxi, rental car, or coach tour.

Soothe Your Spirit

Walk around the cathedral, enjoying its beauty and bounty. Take time to visit the café and the gift shop. Offer a departing prayer of gratitude for God's omnipresence.

A Deeper Look

The visitor's study center, café, and bookshop in the Close were established to share information with tourists, pilgrims, school groups, and others interested in the cathedral, ecclesiastical literature, and the history of Lichfield.

Lincoln Cathedral (Cathedral Church of the Blessed Virgin Mary of Lincoln)◓

Lincoln, Lincolnshire County, England

He giveth power to the faint; and to them
that have no might he increaseth strength.
—Bible, Isaiah 40:29

When Remigius de Fécamp, the first bishop of Lincoln, ordered a cathedral to be built atop a hill facing Lincoln Castle in A.D. 1072, construction began on the Cathedral Church of the Blessed Virgin Mary of Lincoln. In 1092, just two days before the cathedral was to be consecrated, Bishop Remigius died. A fire destroyed the roof in 1141; forty years later, an earthquake all but destroyed the building. The spectacular Gothic cathedral that replaced it— and stands majestically today—is the result of the vision and fortitude of Saint Hugh, the medieval bishop of Lincoln who oversaw its construction but died before its completion.

If you find the collapse of old traditions to be disconcerting or seek inspiration in refashioning or rebuilding your life, visit Lincoln Cathedral to witness how vision and persistence can create something grand and enduring out of ruin.

Soothe Your Spirit

While touring the enormous cathedral, pause before one of the arched stained glass windows in the towering nave to reflect on how faith can sustain you through difficult times and empower you to build anew.

A Deeper Look

Lincoln Cathedral—the seat of the Anglican bishop of Lincoln, Church of England—served as a set in the film version of Dan Brown's bestselling novel *The Da Vinci Code*, which some consider a blasphemous use of this holy site.

Machu Picchu⊕
Urubamba Valley, Peru

Feeling important makes one heavy, clumsy, and vain.
To be a warrior one needs to be light-hearted.
—Carlos Castaneda (1925–1998), Peruvian-born anthropologist

Perched on an emerald-green hilltop rising almost 8,000 feet above sea level and cradled between two craggy peaks of the Peruvian Andes, the famed "Lost City of the Incas" looms above the Urubamba Valley. Upon seeing the mist-enshrouded, fifteenth-century ruin with its remarkably preserved granite structures and terraced fields, travelers describe a sense of awe and intense spiritual power. Unknown to the outside world until 1911 (thus escaping Spanish conquistadores), Machu Picchu (Old Peak) was for centuries a secret Inca ceremonial center, retreat, and perhaps a fortress, and is now a New Age mecca and World Heritage site.

You can journey to Machu Picchu to draw strength from the sacred mountain, the mystical Lost City, and its unspoiled 80,309-acre nature reserve. Go during the dry season, May through September. Wear sunscreen and comfortable walking shoes, take a hat, and explore this 5-square-mile wonder that is roughly 70 miles from Cuzco.

Soothe Your Spirit
As you explore the ruins, feel the spiritual potency of this fiercely beautiful mountaintop sanctuary. At Intihuatana (the Temple of the Sun), in what archaeologists call the "Sacred District" of Machu Picchu, offer a prayer for strength.

A Deeper Look
Machu Picchu, where some believe the energy of the world converges, has an urban section with temples, fountains, palaces, and homes and an agricultural section of terraced gardens (*andenes*).

Mahabodhi Temple of Bodh Gaya✸
Bihar, India

The greatest gift is to give people your enlightenment, to share it.
—Siddhartha Gautama, the Buddha (563–483 B.C.), father of Buddhism

The stupa (bell-shaped tower) of the red-brick Mahabodhi Temple, Buddhism's most sacred shrine, finds resonance in four small towers thrust upward as if to pull the ancient Indian sky to Earth made holy when the Buddha achieved enlightenment under a bodhi tree. A massive gold statue of Buddha in the Earth-touching mudra (symbolic gesture) occupies the temple's inner sanctum as if it had been sitting in that asana (yoga position) for the last 2,500 years since Siddhartha Gautama achieved self-realization and became known as the "Awakened One."

If you desire enlightenment, visit the temple in the village of Bodh Gaya where you can sit, pray, even walk in meditation. The trip from Gaya to Bodh Gaya is 13 miles, easily traveled by a daily deluxe bus service, with time to gather your thoughts before entering the Buddhist sanctuary, visiting the tree, or studying the exquisite images of Buddha carved in the walls.

Soothe Your Spirit
Walk alongside the Cankamana (Cloister Walk) where the footsteps of the Buddha are marked with rounds of carved lotuses to indicate where he walked back and forth in meditation. Inside, study the silk-draped gilded Buddha seated serenely before a turquoise background. In this holy sanctuary, before the altar and ghee lamps, offer heartfelt prayers to develop the compassion of a bodhisattva for those who suffer. Pray for the blessings of the Buddha to guide you in your quest for enlightenment.

A Deeper Look
A section of stone railing from the first century B.C. was added as an enclosure of the small, simple shrine that Emperor Ashoka had built in the third century. You can still make out images of imaginary beasts on the railing medallions.

Mahabodhi Temple of Bodh Gaya, Bihar, India

Mahaparinirvana Temple✺
Kushinagar, Kasia, Uttar Pradesh, India

It is better to conquer yourself than to win a thousand battles.
—Siddhartha Gautama, the Buddha (563–483 B.C.), father of Buddhism

In the temple, a massive bronze statue of Buddha lies on his side as if in the great sleep of *parinirvana* (passing away), draped in shimmering golden ochre (the color of renunciation). Pilgrims from around the world offer prayers of homage and veneration to the Enlightened One at Kushinagar—one of the four sacred sites of pilgrimage specified by the Buddha, along with Lumbini (his birthplace), Bodh Gaya (place of enlightenment), and Sarnath (site of the Buddha's first teaching). If you love the Buddha and his teachings about love, compassion, and liberation (enlightenment), visit the sacred site of his *parinirvana*.

Soothe Your Spirit
Take as much time as you need to absorb the ambiance and subtle sacred energy of the place where Buddha discarded the body he no longer needed. Be open to the inspiration that comes when you pray to the Buddha to help you in your spiritual quest.

A Deeper Look
The ruins of many ancient monasteries are located around the Buddha's Parinirvana Temple at Kushinagar near the border of Nepal.

Mar Elias Monastery✳

Jerusalem, Israel

A good man leaves an inheritance to his children's children,
but the sinner's wealth is laid up for the righteous.
—Bible, Proverbs 13:22

On a ridge with panoramic views of the ancient road between Bethlehem and Jerusalem, the twelfth-century Greek Orthodox monastery of Mar Elias stands like a fortress, in stark contrast to the three-story Byzantine building with a bell tower that once stood on the site. In that original sixth-century church, the prophet Elijah (Elias) found shelter while fleeing the vindictive queen Jezebel. Elijah performed many miracles, including raising a child of a poor widow from the dead. Today, the monastery is a popular pilgrimage site, especially for infertile women and sick and infirm children, who believe that here their prayers are answered.

Whether you seek Elijah's assistance in bringing health to a child or bringing a child into your home, come to Mar Elias. The monastery is 3 miles from central Jerusalem and roughly a mile from the checkpoint into Bethlehem from Jerusalem. Get there by rental car, taxi, or guided tour.

Soothe Your Spirit

Cover you head, light a candle, and pray for the blessing of good homes and good health for all children.

A Deeper Look

A stone bench memorializing the pre-Raphaelite painter William Holman Hunt in front of the monastery reads: "Thou shalt love the lord thy God with all thy heart and with all thy soul, and thy neighbor as thyself" (Bible, Luke 10:27).

Mariazell Basilica
(Basilica of the Birth of Virgin Mary) ◐
Mariazell, Austria

God pardons like a mother, who kisses the
offence into everlasting forgiveness.
—Henry Ward Beecher (1813–1887), Protestant minister and author

The Alpine basilica is easily recognized in the Austrian hamlet of Mariazell because of its Gothic central steeple and twin baroque spires. It has an ornate high altar and a sacred shrine that holds the holy Madonna and Child wooden sculpture, which is said to be miraculous. The church has been a popular pilgrimage site from the twelfth century but especially after a fourteenth-century secular court ordered criminals to make the Mariazell pilgrimage to atone for their crimes.

If you feel the need to atone for something, visit the Mariazell Basilica. The basilica is open November 1 to April 30 from 7:30 a.m. to 7:15 p.m. and May 1 to October 31 from 6:00 a.m. to 8:00 p.m. Fly into Vienna and take the train to St. Polten and then to Mariazell; a bus will take you into the heart of town. Then, walk the short distance remaining. Or, take Route 20 from Vienna southwest to Mariazell, roughly 80 miles.

Soothe Your Spirit
Confess your sin. Attend the celebration of the Mass and receive the sacrament of penance at this center of Austrian pilgrimage. Let spiritual inspiration further guide you to a method of atonement.

A Deeper Look
The Mariazell Basilica is central Europe's most visited Marian shrine. Our Lady of Mariazell is known by many names, including the "Great Mother of the Slavic People" and the "Great Mother of Austria."

Masada ✱
Israel

When you have no choice, mobilize the spirit of courage.
—Jewish proverb

In A.D. 66, Jewish zealots (Sicarii) captured Masada, the virtually impenetrable fortress palace of Herod the Great, built on the summit of a mesa 30 miles southeast of Jerusalem. On that windy butte overlooking the Dead Sea and the Judean Desert, they established the last stronghold of Jewish rule in Palestine. After the fall of Jerusalem and destruction of the Second Temple four years later, the 960 Sicarii refused to surrender to the fifteen thousand Roman soldiers who besieged Masada. Drawing strength from their faith, they held off the invaders for two years before finally choosing death over life under Roman domination and enslavement.

Whether you want to strengthen your faith or to explore the ruins, Masada awaits. Book a day trip (from any of the local hotels). It's at least a two-hour drive from Jerusalem and half an hour from Arad.

Soothe Your Spirit

See the sprawling Judean desert from the crag of Masada at sunrise, as most pilgrims do. Take the Roman ramp, the serpentine Snake Path, or cable car to the summit and watch the sun rise spectacularly over the desert. Whisper a prayer for the courage and strength to remain true to your faith.

A Deeper Look

The remains of a synagogue built by the Sicarii still stand at Masada as do the palace Herod built, a couple of mikvahs (ritual baths), a church built by fifth-century monks, and other ruins.

Mezquita-Catedral (Mosque-Cathedral)●
Córdoba, Spain

When you see the storm coming, if you seek safety in that firm refuge which is Mary, there will be no danger of your wavering or going down.
—Saint Josemaría Escrivá (1902–1975),
Spanish Roman Catholic priest and founder of Opus Dei

The Mosque-Cathedral of Córdoba began around A.D. 600 as a Visigoth monastery, which the Umayyad Moors converted to a mosque in the late eighth century. About one hundred years later, the Moors built the new Great Mosque on the site, which the Roman Catholic Church reclaimed and consecrated to Saint Mary of the Assumption in 1236. In 1523, the Córdoba diocese removed the center of the mosque and inserted a lavishly ornamented cathedral. Today, this World Heritage site stands as a monument to spiritual strength, both Muslim and Christian.

If you seek strength to deal with a radical change in your life or if you just want to experience a sacred site that has endured centuries of change, visit the Mezquita-Catedral. The nearest airports are Málaga and Seville, and the Córdoba Railway Station links to cities in Spain. In the city, hail a taxi, ride the local bus, or take a guided tour.

Soothe Your Spirit
Envision sustaining your spiritual equilibrium as you lean into the change you face or desire. Offer a prayer of gratitude to Mary for her strength in delivering her only Son to the world, that all may go forth in strength.

A Deeper Look
Mezquita-Catedral stands on a sacred site of pagan Roman worship, where a Roman temple to Janus once existed.

Milk Grotto✲

Bethlehem, Israel

To hope means to be ready at every moment for that which is not yet born,
and yet not become desperate if there is no birth in our lifetime.
—Erich Fromm (1900–1980), German-American Jewish psychologist and philosopher

The Milk Grotto, a holy shrine venerated by Muslims and Christians and dedicated to Our Lady of the Milk, safeguards a rock that purportedly was formed from a few drops of milk that fell from the Blessed Virgin's breast as she nursed the Holy Infant. The grotto, also believed to have been a place of hiding for the Holy Family during the Slaughter of the Innocents decreed by Herod, sheds a limestone dust that the faithful have pinched and taken with them in the hope of experiencing fertility through ritual use.

If you desire fertility but have lost hope, visit the Milk Grotto to ask for help from Our Lady of the Milk. Take a day trip (by rental car) to Bethlehem from the West Bank of Jerusalem.

Soothe Your Spirit

Pray for the fertility you desire. If you feel inspired, you might also purchase a small packet of the "milk" limestone powder from the Franciscans, complete with directions for use.

A Deeper Look

Although the Grotto is two thousand years old, pilgrims have prayed at the site for fertility since the fourth century, and nuns pray around the clock in shifts behind a glass screen in the grotto. According to a 2007 CNS report, 1,700 babies were born to parents who had prayed at the shrine over the previous ten years.

Mono Lake⬤

Mono Lake Tufa State Natural Reserve, Mono Lake County, California, United States

The trees reflected in the river—they are unconscious of a spiritual world so near to them. So are we.
—Nathaniel Hawthorne (1804–1864), American fiction writer

Mono Lake, formed eons before humans walked on Earth, is a sacred site to diverse groups of people, from Native American tribes to conservationists, New Age believers, and practitioners of Wicca, Animism, and Paganism. This Northern California lake fed by runoff water has no outlet (such as a river, stream, or ocean) and high salinity. The combination has created a fertile ecosystem that supports brine shrimp, which, in turn, feed more than two million migratory birds.

If evidence of Creation's ancient fertility might invigorate fertility in your spiritual, creative, charitable, or vocational endeavors, visit Mono Lake. The lake sits right on Highway 395 between the towns of Mono City and Lee Vining (which has a small airport) on the eastern side of Northern California near the Nevada border.

Soothe Your Spirit

Take a guided nature hike to learn about this ancient place of fertility so revered by many spiritual traditions. Cast a sacred circle and invoke the Goddess to inspire you with ideas on how to be more fertile in all areas of your life.

A Deeper Look

In December 2010, NASA scientists discovered a new life form in Mono Lake: the rod-shaped bacterium GFAJ-1, an extremophile that is not adversely affected by arsenic, which is poisonous to many living creatures.

Mother Cathedral of Holy Etchmiadzin✷

Vagharshapat, Armenia

But Noah found grace in the eyes of the Lord.
—Bible, Genesis 6:8

The Etchmiadzin Cathedral, world headquarters of the Holy Armenian Apostolic Church, is the most visited pilgrimage destination in Armenia by Orthodox Christians. The fourth-century A.D. buff-colored, angular church has three towers capped with crosses, a fifth-century dome, and a softly lit Byzantine interior adorned with sacred art. This ancient holy site was once home to a Zoroastrian fire temple and then a temple of Venus under the Romans. In the early fourth century, a Christian church was built by Saint Gregory the Illuminator, after he experienced a numinous vision of the Holy Spirit, in which Christ descended with a golden hammer to show him where to build a church that would shelter the Armenian faithful for centuries to come. The cathedral safeguards holy relics such as the sword that pierced Jesus' side and a piece of wood that has been carbon-dated to six thousand years and is believed to be from Noah's Ark.

If you are seeking God's safekeeping, visit Etchmiadzin Cathedral to be reminded that even in the Great Flood, God protected Noah, his family, and the animals in the Ark. The cathedral is located about 15 miles from Yerevan in the town of Vagharshapat.

Soothe Your Spirit

Light a candle and pray that just as the Holy Spirit descended upon Saint Gregory, you, too, might be sheltered and safeguarded in your passage through life.

A Deeper Look

Frescoes from biblical scenes and saintly figures adorn the interior of this magnificent World Heritage site, believed to be the oldest cathedral in the world.

Mother Cathedral of Holy Etchmiadzin, Vagharshapat, Armenia

Mount Croagh Patrick ◈
County Mayo, Ireland

Before I was humiliated I was like a stone that lies in deep mud,
and he who is mighty came and in his compassion raised me up
and exalted me very high and placed me on the top of the wall.
—Saint Patrick (ca. A.D. 387–493), Christian missionary and bishop

When English missionary Patrick desired to fast and pray in solitude during the season of Lent in preparation for Easter, he climbed the cone-shaped mountain that rises from the verdant plain of County Mayo and stayed up there for forty days and nights. Legend says he banished the snakes from Ireland while on that mountain and, before descending, threw down a silver cup that turned black, symbolically gathering all the blackness from Ireland into that vessel.

If you feel the urge for penance and seek spiritual redemption and wholeness, walk Mount Croagh Patrick, Ireland's most important holy site of pilgrimage. Travel to Westport by train, bus, or car from Dublin or Galway. Westport is 5 miles from the mountain.

Soothe Your Spirit

Stop at each of the three marked stations on your ascent and pray, make declarations, or perform spiritual rituals as suggested on the signs. If your beliefs differ from Judeo-Christian, take time to honor your beliefs. At the summit, enter the small white chapel to reflect. Then ask forgiveness for any unkind thoughts and actions and forgive others to make things right with the Higher Power in your life.

A Deeper Look

Roughly a million people reach the top of Mount Croagh Patrick each year, with close to half that number climbing the mountain the last Sunday in July, some on their knees.

Mount Desert Island ❦
Maine, United States

*Courage and honor endure forever. Their echoes remain
when the mountains have crumbled to dust.*
—Wiccan Code of Chivalry

Maine's spectacular Mount Desert Island with its crashing waves, sparkling waterways, forested mountains, craggy coastline, granite cliffs, and invigorating sea air became a refuge in the nineteenth century for wealthy families seeking solace and respite. For the indigenous Wabanaki (People of the Dawnland), the island they know as Pemetic (the sloping land) was sacred. For practitioners of Wicca and other Earth-based spiritual traditions, the island's wild beauty has ideal places to cast sacred circles for gathering spiritual strength.

To spend time in a restorative natural setting, you can't beat Mount Desert Island, home to Acadia National Park. The best time to visit is mid- to late summer. Drive to the island town of Bar Harbor from Bangor or Boston.

Soothe Your Spirit
Take a reflective stroll along a coastal path or one of the historical carriage roads used by walkers. Find a quiet spot and cast a magical stone circle. Commune with the energy of this island sanctuary and give voice to your desire or intention. Offer prayers of declaration, courage, and gratitude.

A Deeper Look
Mount Desert has only four towns, and yet the island accommodates more than two and a half million tourists annually. The island's Cadillac Mountain is the tallest on the eastern seacoast and where the sunrise is first seen in the United States.

Mount Diablo☯

Clayton, California, United States

Climb the mountains and get their good tidings. Nature's peace will flow into you as sunshine flows into trees...cares will drop off like autumn leaves.
—John Muir (1838–1914), Scottish-born American naturalist

The Miwok and Ohlone tribes centered their creation myths on this isolated mountain towering 3,864 feet between the San Francisco Bay and California's Central Valley. For Wicca and New Age practitioners, this mountain heals and rejuvenates those who spend time exploring its wild woodlands, arid grasslands, and rocky ridgelines. If you seek spiritual, emotional, or physical healing or nourishment, take a day to experience this natural sanctuary. You can reach the mountain and 20,000-acre park by car from anywhere in the Bay Area. Park hours are 8:00 a.m. to sunset. Alcohol and fireworks are prohibited.

Soothe Your Spirit

Take your prayer rug and find a scenic spot where you can sit undisturbed. Invite a companion to join you (if you are concerned about personal safety). Listen to nature's sounds. Breathe in the scents and imagine that each of your inward breaths carries energy imbued with the mountain's strength. Affirm in each cycle of breath that you are being revitalized, healed, and made whole.

A Deeper Look

In 1805, according to legend, Spanish soldiers searching for Native Americans who had escaped from a mission during the night got caught in thick brush on the mountain, proclaiming *"monte del Diablo"* ("forest or thicket of the Devil"), which sounded like Mount Diablo.

Mount Kailash ✵
Western Tibet, China

This is my simple religion. There is no need for temples;
no need for complicated philosophy. Our own brain, our
own heart is our temple; the philosophy is kindness.
—Dalai Lama (1935–), Tibetan spiritual leader

S acred to four faiths—Hindu, Buddhist, Jain, and Bon—the incomparable Mount Kailash juts 22,028 feet out of the Himalayas in western Tibet as a spectacular jewel. Its snowcapped peak glistens in the light at the rooftop of the world, beckoning the faithful to come, walk, reflect, pray, and find peace. Annually, thousands of pilgrims answer that call, believing that circumambulating the mountain bestows blessings and abolishes sin.

If you feel a spiritual connection to mountains and believe that time spent in a meditative walk would nurture your spirit, and you are physically able to do the arduous walking and tent camping, make a pilgrimage to Mount Kailash. The easiest way is to book an all-inclusive tour from Kathmandu or Lhasa; however, the trek begins and ends in the city of Darchen. The best time to go is May through September when the weather is more hospitable.

Soothe Your Spirit

Make your pilgrimage a devotional walk, focus on engaging the mind in prayer, recitation of a mantra, or reflection; or, quietly hum or sing spiritual chants or sacred songs.

A Deeper Look

The Kailash pilgrim's circuit will take about three days to walk; it stretches 32 miles. Hindus and Buddhists circumambulate the mountain in a clockwise direction, while followers of the Bon and Jain trek it in a counterclockwise direction.

Mount Olympus⬢

Thessaloniki, Greece

[Odysseus weeps] as a woman weeps when she throws her arms round the body of her beloved husband, fallen in battle before his city and his comrades, fighting to save his home-town and his children from disaster.
—Homer (800–700 B.C.), *The Iliad*, Greek epic poet

Spectacular Mount Olympus rises regally above the clouds in central Greece, silently blessing those seeking the treasure of its peace. In the classical Greek and Hellenistic worlds, the mountain was known as "the home of the Gods," where Zeus, king of Olympus and the supreme deity, resided with his Divine family.

If you seek serenity and strength, visit the sanctuary of Zeus and let the breathtaking beauty of the mountain permeate your being with restorative healing. Catch a bus or train from Athens or Thessaloniki to Litochoro at the base of Mount Olympus, and rise early to see the mountain blaze awake with the fiery colors of crimson and ginger.

Soothe Your Spirit

Hike to the summit to feel the breath of those ancient gods caressing you as the breezes blow. Affirm the richness of life. Pray for someone you have lost or for strength and serenity to deal with the loss.

A Deeper Look

Mount Olympus rises a spectacular 9,577 feet near the Thermaic Gulf on the Aegean Sea and borders Thessaly and Macedonia. Often snowcapped, the mountain, with its fifty-two peaks, frequently has cloud cover despite Homer's observation, in his epic poem *The Odyssey*, that it never has storms but basks in cloudless ether.

Mount Shasta⌔

Shasta City, California, United States

Doubt makes the mountain which faith can move.
—Proverb

S acred to numerous Native American tribes, more than one hundred New
Age sects, the Rosicrucian Order, and a Buddhist monastery, this holy
mountain at the southern end of the Cascades straddles the California-Oregon
border and has been continually inhabited for nine thousand years. Today,
more than a New Age mecca, it might be more appropriately described as a
holy New Age epicenter following the Harmonic Convergence of 1987 when
more than five thousand spiritual people from around the world gathered to
pray and meditate on world peace.

If you want to transform yourself or the world, visit Mount Shasta to jump-
start the process. Take Highway 5 to the city of Mount Shasta and pick up
Everitt Memorial Highway to Bunny Flat Trailhead. There, at 6,860 feet, enter
onto trails to the summit, or enjoy the verdant meadows (in summer) and the
shimmering waterfalls.

To enter the wilderness areas, you will need a permit; contact the Mount
Shasta Ranger Station at (530) 926-4511 for information on getting a permit.

Soothe Your Spirit

Hike the mountain trails until you
find a place where you'd like to
meditate upon the mountain that
New Age practitioners believe is
a sacred energy vortex. Tune into
Earth's energy and dive deeply into
meditation, opening your heart to
messages, inspiration, or changes.

A Deeper Look

Mount Shasta supports more than
four hundred species of wildlife.

Mount Tai Shan✳

Tai'an, Shandong Province, China

When you realize there is nothing lacking; the whole world belongs to you.
—Lao Tzu (600–531 B.C.), Chinese philosopher and father of Taoism

Tai Shan, holiest of China's five sacred mountain peaks, offers views of majestic peaks, shimmering waterfalls, deep gorges, ancient groves of pine and cypress, and verdant valleys. The four routes to the top of Tai Shan abound with cultural relics and majestic scenery whose names speak to a long relationship with deity: Jade Emperor Summit, Eight Immortals Cave, and Heaven and Earth Square. Humans have left their traces on this holy mountain since the Paleolithic period, four hundred thousand years ago.

If you seek a fertile mind or body, offer prayers to Songzi Niangniang, goddess of fertility, one of several deities venerated in the Azure Cloud Temple. Walk there on the Peach Blossom Ravine Route in springtime, when breezes carrying blossoms impart an even deeper spiritual ambiance. Take 104 National Highway to the shuttle bus area, and then continue on the bus to the cable car station at Midway Gate to Heaven. The cable car takes you to the top in a few minutes.

Soothe Your Spirit

Improvise on an ancient tradition: take a small shot glass and place it in the sun, add water, place your hands over the glass, and pray for fertility (thus imbuing the water with spirit before drinking it). Light a stick of incense so the curling tendril of smoke carries your prayer into heaven. Leave the glass in the sun when you've finished; the sun's rays energize the water.

A Deeper Look

Tai Shan's main peak rises 5,068 feet (1,545 meters) above sea level.

Mount Tai Shan, Tai'an, Shandong Province, China

Museum Our Lord in the Attic
(formerly Museum Amstelkring)◓

Amsterdam, Netherlands

*Certain thoughts are prayers. There are moments when,
whatever be the attitude of the body, the soul is on its knees.*
—Victor Hugo (1802–1885), French playwright and novelist

In 1661, wealthy merchant Jan Hartman purchased property in Amsterdam and created, in his home, a sacred sanctuary that included a magnificent altarpiece, *Baptism of Christ* (1716), by Jacob de Wit, marble columns, and sculptures of angels. Even though Catholicism was banned in Amsterdam in 1578, Hartman's love for his faith compelled him to allocate the top story of his dignified home as a Catholic church, hidden from view.

If you desire to deepen your religious beliefs, visit the church that one man's love for his faith built during a time of religious persecution, but know that the stairs to reach the church are quite steep.

Museum Our Lord in the Attic is located at Oudezijds Voorburgwal 40. Fly to Amsterdam Airport Schiphol and take a taxi, bus, or rental car to the church. It is also a short walk from Central Station/Damrak.

Soothe Your Spirit

Take at least an hour to see everything. Answer the question: what can I do, inwardly and outwardly, to deepen my love for my faith and to put my love into actions that will benefit others? Follow your answers with an action list.

A Deeper Look

Museum Our Lord in the Attic served Amsterdam's Catholic community for two hundred years before other churches were built.

National Cathedral●
Washington, DC, United States

Death is not the greatest loss in life; the greatest loss is what dies inside us while we live.
—Norman Cousins (1912–1990), American essayist

A merica's Episcopalian National Cathedral with its lofty vaulted ceiling, exquisite stained glass windows, exhibit of state flags, exterior flying buttresses, elegant carvings, and statuary, fulfilled Pierre L'Enfant's vision to create a grand house of prayer for national purposes. The cathedral has served as the sanctuary for the nation's final goodbyes to nearly all of the twenty-one United States presidents since Congress approved the cathedral's charter in 1893.

If you want to say a final goodbye to a friend, a leader of our nation, someone in service, or someone working for a community's greater good, visit the National Cathedral. Located at 3101 Wisconsin Avenue NW, in Washington, DC, the easiest way to get there is by car from downtown. Take Massachusetts Avenue north to Wisconsin and turn right. The cathedral sits on the right.

Soothe Your Spirit

Sink into the peace of this national house of worship that welcomes people of all faiths. Let your heart mourn its loss and say a final prayer of goodbye. Go home and plant some forget-me-nots in a pot with some soil in honor of your loved one. The flowers come back year after year.

A Deeper Look

In keeping with the medieval belief that only God is perfect, the cathedral was built with flaws of intentional asymmetry.

Newgrange Passage Tomb⬢
County Meath, Slane, Ireland

When we quit thinking primarily about ourselves and our self-preservation,
we undergo a truly heroic transformation of consciousness.
—Joseph Campbell (1904–1987), American mythologist, writer, and lecturer

About 3100 B.C., prehistoric inhabitants of Ireland created the Newgrange Passage Tomb, a sacred stone circle with a passage leading to a burial chamber similar to other ancient stone circles that align the circle's axis to the solstices. Here, a roof box allows the winter solstice's sunlight to align precisely with the center of the tomb's passageway. This sacred site might have been an ancient temple with ceremonial importance, but it has upright stones that are richly decorated in triple spirals, and outside the tomb, twelve of thirty-five stones that once may have encircled the massive turf-covered mound remain with a solitary carved kerbstone at the entrance.

If you feel a connection to Celtic beliefs or a reverence for Earth, come to see the Newgrange Passage Tomb. Visits to Newgrange are by guided tour only from Brú na Bóinne Visitors Center, located on the south side of the River Boyne 1.2 miles west of Donore. To get to Donore, take the M1 heading north and exit at Donore, near Drogheda, and follow the signs.

Soothe Your Spirit
Find a stone that you feel attracted to; use it as a talisman to remind you that transformation can take millennia or it can happen in an instant.

A Deeper Look
Archaeologists say it probably took hundreds of people working twenty years or more to build Newgrange. The site is older than the Pyramid of Giza and approximately one thousand years older than Stonehenge.

Normandy American Cemetery⬬
Colleville-sur-Mer, France

I give unto them eternal life and they shall never perish.
—Chapel inscription, Normandy American Cemetery

When the fighting was over in Normandy at the end of World War II, the battlefield there had hundreds of small burial grounds, more than ten American cemeteries, and numerous isolated graves of Americans who had fallen on French soil. Roughly 60 percent of the burials were repatriated to the United States; the remaining casualties were divided between the Brittany cemetery and the 172.5-acre Normandy cemetery. In this cemetery rest four women, three Medal of Honor recipients, and thirty-three pairs of brothers buried side by side, including the two who inspired the movie *Saving Private Ryan*.

Whether you are a veteran interested in military history, lost a loved one in this war, or would like to say a prayer for the 9,387 soldiers who fell here, visit the Normandy American Cemetery. It is located at 14710 Colleville-sur-Mer, France, and is regularly open until 5:00 p.m. Visit the website: www.abmc.gov/cemeteries-memorials/europe/normandy-american-cemetery. If your loved one is buried in this cemetery, this website will also help you find the location of the grave.

Soothe Your Spirit
Pass the memorial, the Garden of Missing, and follow the path to the chapel. Reflect on the service given to our country by those young men and women, perhaps your relative among them. Pray for eternal peace for their souls and for the safety of all the men and women serving the cause of freedom today.

A Deeper Look
The cemetery paths are laid out in a Latin cross, and there is a viewing platform of Omaha Beach where the 1st Division landed on D-Day.

Normandy American Cemetery, Colleville-sur-Mer, France

Norwich Cathedral⬤
Norwich, Norfolk, England

All shall be well, and all shall be well,
and all manner of thing shall be well.
—Julian of Norwich (1342–1416), English mystic

As if the astonishing beauty and enormous size of the nine-hundred-year-old Norwich Cathedral in eastern England weren't enough to draw pilgrims over the Atlantic and across the English Channel, its rich chorale music, treasury of sacred art, labyrinth, verdant gardens, and enthusiastic welcome to people of all faiths surely add to the allure. This Romanesque cathedral where open-armed spiritual succor is a governing principle draws tens of thousands of worshippers every year.

Whether you would like to learn more about the cathedral's Benedictine heritage and historical medieval buildings or give your spirit a boost, Norwich Cathedral will inform and inspire you. Located in the heart of Norwich, the cathedral is best reached by taxi or public transportation; parking in the Close is not permitted, except in special cases of disability if you've made previous arrangements.

Soothe Your Spirit

Light a candle and pray silently that your heart may find comfort, your mind may find peace, and your soul may find guidance.

A Deeper Look

Among the religious figures commemorated at Norwich Cathedral are Herbert de Losinga, the Norman monk who was the first bishop of Norwich and founded the church in A.D. 1096, and Julian of Norwich, who "exemplifies the very best in the English mystic tradition of the fourteenth century and lay ministry at its most refined." Dame Julian's birth name is unknown; she is named for the church at which she lived as an anchoress, or hermit.

Old Ship Church●
Hingham, Massachusetts, United States

Some rise by sin, and some by virtue fall.
—William Shakespeare (1564–1616), English playwright and poet

When the Puritans built the Old Ship Meetinghouse in 1681 amid rolling verdant hills on the easternmost flank of coastal Massachusetts, they created in their sacred sanctuary a Gothic timber ceiling that resembles the inverted hull of a ship. Now a Unitarian Universalist church, the site showcases a framed 1680s seating chart, and Hingham Cemetery, sometimes called the First Settlers Cemetery, a colonial graveyard filled with centuries-old markers and headstones of upstanding pilgrims and the less notable who surely took secrets and sins to the grave as humans always have.

Whether you have a grudge, a secret, or a sin you'd like to bury, begin the process by attending a worship service in Old Ship Church. It's located at 107 Main Street. Hingham is located between Cohasset and Weymouth off of Highway 3A, just inland from Massachusetts Bay.

Soothe Your Spirit

Ask Divine forgiveness for yourself or others involved in the burden you carry. Write on paper a sentence forgiving yourself and others. Visit the cemetery with a vow not to take the burden with you to the grave. When you are alone, burn the paper; do not mentally revisit what your conscience has cleared.

A Deeper Look

Old Ship Church is considered the oldest surviving Puritan meetinghouse in North America and the only continuous ecclesiastical house of worship with regular services still offered.

Our Lady of Częstochowa (Black Madonna)●
Monastery of Jasna Góra, Częstochowa, Jasna Góra, Poland

Madonna, Black Madonna, in her arms
you will find peace...and be protected...
—Polish song, "Black Madonna"

In 1650, Grand Chancellor George Ossoliński was so inspired by the Black Madonna of Częstochowa that he made as his votive offering an ebony and silver altar. Today, the altar and the much-revered painting—said to have been painted by Saint Luke the Evangelist on a tabletop made by Jesus—are enshrined in the small fifteenth-century Gothic chapel adjoining the majestic sixteenth-century baroque monastery of Jasna Góra. Many miracles are credited to the icon of the Black Madonna, including the safety of Jasna Góra during threatened invasions in the seventeenth century by the Swedes and later in the twentieth century by the Nazis. Today, millions of Christians from around the world come to Our Lady of Częstochowa, whose images of Madonna and Child have blackened from centuries of votive smoke.

Whether you seek safe passage during your sacred travels or protection from religious oppression, visit the Black Madonna of Jasna Góra. Located in south-central Poland, Częstochowa can be reached from all major cities by rail, bus, or rental car.

Soothe Your Spirit
Light a candle, pray for what you wish to safeguard, and leave a votive offering.

A Deeper Look
In 1430, a thief twice slashed the Black Madonna with his sword. As he raised his arm to deliver a third gash, he purportedly fell to the ground in pain and died. The icon still bears the scars of that defacement.

Our Lady of the Spasm Church✸
Jerusalem, Israel

And there followed him a great company of people,
and of women, which also bewailed and lamented him.
—Bible, Luke 23:27

After falling under the weight of the heavy wooden cross (Station 3 on the Via Dolorosa), Jesus met his mother (Station 4) at the site of Our Lady of the Spasm, just behind the walls lining a short section of the Via Dolorosa. This modest Armenian Orthodox church was built in the sixteenth century, and its chapel, located in the crypt, displays several evocative paintings of Jesus. A fifth-century floor mosaic survives in which the Holy Mother's footprints are represented as sandals.

Coming to terms with loss is a process that could begin at this site. Getting around Jerusalem is fairly easy using local transportation. You could also take a local tour and walk.

Soothe Your Spirit
Read the passage about Jesus' counsel to his mother and his women followers. Reflect on why he told them not to weep, and consider the possibility that belief in a higher power in times of darkness may bring comfort when nothing else can and help you embrace life.

A Deeper Look
Although the New Testament is silent about Jesus and Mary meeting along the Via Dolorosa, popular tradition supports the story, and a lunette (a half-moon-shaped space) over the church doorway commemorates the meeting in a bas-relief.

Pamukkale (Hierapolis) ✱
Denizli Province, Turkey

The drop dies in the river / of its joy / pain goes so far it cures itself...
—Ghalib (1797–1869), Turkish poet, trans. W.S. Merwin

In an arid landscape the color of camels, Pamukkale (Cotton Palace) is a refreshing ancient thermal spa with mineral-rich waters that for millennia have tumbled down Caldag Mountain, leaving behind white travertine terraces. Here, too, are the ruins of Hierapolis (Holy City), a Greco-Roman community and religious retreat founded in the second century B.C. and later converted to Christianity by Philip the Apostle. The ruins include a cathedral, a baptistery, churches, and the tomb of the apostle Philip, who died there in A.D. 80.

Nestled in a surreal landscape of mineral forests, terraced basins, and petrified waterfalls, Pamukkale's sacred warm water can baptize the spirit, soothe the soul, and restore a weary body. Sitting and wading (shoes prohibited) is free, but you must pay to swim. You can reach Hierapolis-Pamukkale from Denizli, the nearest city, by car or local bus, but be sure to go early as the tour buses bring large crowds.

Soothe Your Spirit
Bathe in the springs as the faithful have been doing for thousands of years. Release all your worry and concerns. Pray for the restoration of perfect health in body, mind, and spirit, and offer a prayer of heartfelt thanks.

A Deeper Look
Since before the birth of Christ, the sick and infirm have come from far and wide to bathe in the warm waters of Hierapolis-Pamukkale, which are believed to have mystical healing powers.

Panagia Ekatontapyliani Church⬢
Pirikia, Paros, Greece

If you are very valiant, it is a god, I think, who gave you this gift.
—Homer (800–700 B.C.), *The Iliad*, Greek epic poet

This fourth-century A.D. Orthodox Church complex, whose name means Our Lady of a Hundred Doors, is the oldest Byzantine Christian church in Greece. In 1962, a renowned Greek scholar confirmed Saint Helen and her son, the Roman emperor Constantine, as the founders of this marble monument venerating four saints (Anargiron, Philip, Theodosia, and Dimitrios) and a ninth-century nun, Osia Theoktisti. According to legend, pirates kidnapped several young nuns from a convent on Lesbos, and when they docked at Pirikia, which was deserted due to the frequent pirate raids, to allow the nuns to recover from seasickness, Osia escaped into the woods and hid in the abandoned church. She lived alone for thirty-five years, subsisting on wild plants and holy water.

If you wish to pay homage to Osia's bravery or to restore your faith, visit Our Lady of a Hundred Doors. From Athens, Mykonos, or Santorini, take a ferry to Paros, in the Cyclades Island group. Alternatively, you can take a small plane from Athens to Paros.

Soothe Your Spirit
Let the holy vibration of this elegant church strengthen your faith. In Osia's chapel, near where her relics are entombed, offer a prayer of gratitude for Divine protection.

A Deeper Look
There is evidence that a temple existed on the site as early as A.D. 326, where Saint Helen may have taken refuge during a storm while on a mission to find the Holy Cross.

Panagia Ekatontapyliani Church, Pirikia, Paros, Greece

Panagia Gorgoepikoos
(Church of Our Lady Who Hears Swiftly)◉
Pláka, Athens, Greece

Before, by yourself, you couldn't. Now, you've turned to
Our Lady, and with her, how easy!
—Saint Josemaría Escrivá (1902–1975), Spanish Roman
Catholic priest and founder of Opus Dei

The tiny church of Panagia Gorgoepikoos is revered by Athenians for its icon of Theotokos (the Mother of God), to whom many miracles have been attributed, including swift responses to petitions. The lower walls of this elegant cross-in-square church are constructed of unadorned marble. In contrast, the upper portions display ninety bas-reliefs, replete with pagan symbols—remnants of an ancient temple razed to build the church—that were Christianized with the insertion of crosses.

Whether you want to make a supplication before the holy icon or to see and learn more about this historic church, pay a visit to Panagia Gorgoepikoos. It is located at Plateía Mitropóleos, adjacent to the Mitrópoli. Take a taxi or the metro rail (get off at the metro stops for Syntagma or Monastiráki).

Soothe Your Spirit
Offer your prayer before the icon, petitioning Mother Mary to assist you in your quest for Divine understanding and nurturance.

A Deeper Look
The Church of Panagia Gorgoepikoos served as the National Library from 1841 (after the foundation of Greece as a state) until 1863, when its use as a church was restored and it was rededicated to Saint Eleftherios, venerated for his pastoral virtues. The ancient temple from which the church's friezes were repurposed was founded by Athenian-born empress Irene, credited with restoring the Greek Orthodox veneration of icons.

Pashupatinath Temple❋
Kathmandu, Nepal

Om Namah Shivaya.
—Ancient Sanskrit mantra dedicated to Shiva

The square pagoda-style Pashupatinath Temple, built over an older temple dating to the ninth century A.D., has been erected and razed several times. Still it remains the holiest pilgrimage site for Nepalese Hindus; devotees descend the temple's ancient stone steps daily to immerse themselves in the sacred Bagmati River. Dedicated to Lord Shiva (Hindu god of destruction), every inch of the temple astonishes visitors with its beauty: carved lattice windows from Bhutanese monasteries, a gold-plated roof, jewel-embellished doors, spectacular floral motifs carved in wood, and an inner sanctum where the four-sided 3-foot-tall lingam (phallus) of Lord Shiva is venerated.

If you have experienced the end of a relationship, desire reconciliation, or feel as though your life needs a major shift in a new direction, go to the incomparable Pashupatinath Temple that honors Shiva, who oversees the breaking down of old structures so that new ones can be created (Shiva's lingam or phallus symbolizes generative power). Access to the temple interior is for Hindus only, but there are areas open to tourists and visitors.

Soothe Your Spirit
Travel to this World Heritage site on the "rooftop of the world" and find a quiet place to say a prayer for forgiveness or reconciliation.

A Deeper Look
Thousands of Hindu pilgrims visit the temple daily, but during festivals dedicated to Shiva, the crowds grow large. During the annual Maha Shivaratri, the temple remains open all night to accommodate ochre-clad sadhus (or mystics), devotees, pilgrims, and tourists from Nepal and elsewhere in the world.

Peace Memorial✷
Hiroshima Peace Memorial Park, Hiroshima-shi, Hiroshima Prefecture, Japan

Rest in peace, for the error shall not be repeated.
—Inscription on the Hiroshima Peace Memorial Park cenotaph

The Hiroshima Prefectural Industrial Promotion Hall, a four-tiered building with a wire dome crown, escaped the atomic bombs dropped in 1945 even though it was only a few yards from ground zero. The building's dome (referred to by some as the "Atomic Dome") is a bookend for the other memorial on the opposite side of the park—an inverted U-shaped cenotaph bearing the names of the dead.

Whether your ancestry is Japanese or you would like to pray at this site, come to Hiroshima Peace Memorial Park located at 1–2 Nakajimacho, Naka-ku, Hiroshima-shi (Hiroshima City), Hiroshima-ken, Japan. It is open daily, except December 30–31. The Hiroshima International Airport is about 31 miles east of the city. Hiring a taxi is the easiest way to get to the site.

Soothe Your Spirit
Visit the park on the anniversary of the bombing. On August 6 at 8:15 a.m., the moment of detonation, join others in the observed moment of silence to honor those who lost their lives, those who are maimed, and those whose lives will never be the same. Pray for peace.

A Deeper Look
The Hiroshima Memorial Museum was established in 1955 and also includes a memorial for the children who died in the bombing. Despite objections by China and the United States, the Hiroshima Peace Memorial was listed in 1996 on the World Heritage List.

Peace Memorial, Hiroshima Peace Memorial Park,
Hiroshima-shi, Hiroshima Prefecture, Japan

Père Lachaise Cemetery⬣

Paris, France

Have courage for the great sorrows of life and patience for
the small ones; and when you have laboriously accomplished
your daily task, go to sleep in peace. God is awake.
—Victor Hugo (1802–1885), French playwright and novelist

A walk through the beautiful and serene Père Lachaise, amid broad, leafy trees, moss-encrusted headstones, gleaming marble busts, stoic stone cherubs, columned temples, ornate crosses, marble statues of children, legions of angels, and red roses everywhere, can be a soul-soothing and spiritually moving experience. This special cemetery that Parisians call the "City of the Dead" is notable for the famous people interred in its hallowed ground, including the tragic lovers Abelard and Héloïse, Chopin, Édith Piaf, Colette, Marcel Proust, Honoré de Balzac, Alice B. Toklas, Yves Montand, and Jim Morrison. Père Lachaise has served as the model for the gardens found in rural cemeteries of the United States since about 1831.

If you feel that cemeteries serve as a spiritual link to the past or you would like to venerate a departed soul buried in Père Lachaise, embark on a trip to Paris. The main entrance is located at Rue de Repos.

Soothe Your Spirit

Walk through the cemetery and feel the peace in your heart. If there is someone with whom you would like to commune, invite that person's spirit to be present with you, inspiring you as you explore. Offer a prayer for that departed soul.

A Deeper Look

If you're seeking a closer connection to these tranquil grounds, read "Soliloquy in the Cemetery of Père Lachaise" by French poet Jean Garrigue, who the *Saturday Review* called, "undeniably original and individual as an artist, and a craftsman in complete command of her medium." Garrigue captures the cemetery's eerie beauty and its unique effect on those who visit.

Petra✱
Wadi Araba, Jordan

What you leave behind is not what is engraved in stone monuments, but what is woven into the lives of others.
—Pericles (495–429 B.C.), Greek politician

P etra's ornate carvings in pink sandstone glisten under shafts of brilliant sunlight, showcasing the ornamented facade of the two-thousand-year-old Al-Khazneh (the City Treasury) in the dark canyons of southern Jordan. In a landscape where you might expect to see Bedouins tending their sheep or a camel caravan ambling past, the spectacular Treasury and other amazing structures carved by ancient Arabs, the nomadic Nabataeans, might seem like a mirage—or perhaps a miracle of human ingenuity and prosperity.

If you seek creative inspiration or spiritual enrichment, journey to this sacred treasure. Petra is 162 miles south of Amman (Queen Alia International Airport) and 82 miles north of Aqaba in a mountainous desert between the Red Sea and the Mediterranean Sea. Take a guided coach tour to Petra. Once there, stop at the visitors center. Walk (or hire a horse-drawn carriage) to traverse the *siq* (canyon) into the ancient city, and then hire a horse, camel, or donkey to tour the ruins. Wear comfortable walking shoes, loose conservative clothing, and a hat, and bring bottled drinking water.

Soothe Your Spirit
Find inspiration in the brilliant work of the ancient Nabataeans, and bring along a journal to capture your impressions and inspirations.

A Deeper Look
Petra has been inhabited since prehistoric times and was a flourishing trading center when the Nabataeans masterfully executed their elaborate carvings.

Pipestone National Monument ☯
Minnesota, United States

When you pray with this pipe, you pray for and with everything.
—Black Elk (1863–1950), Oglala Lakota Sioux medicine man

The Plains Indians of Minnesota describe the sacred Pipestone Quarry, named a United States Historical National Monument in 1937, as a "square jewel" because from a distance it looks like a giant square-cut ruby. Today, only Native Americans are allowed to quarry the catlinite, the red stone used to carve pipes for medicinal and peace ceremonies as well as for communing with the spirit world.

If you embrace the Native American belief that smoke from the sacred calumet (the pipe made from pipestone or catlinite) carries prayers for well-being to the Great Spirit, visit this national monument that has been sacred to indigenous people for thousands of years. The best time is late spring, early summer, or fall. Located in southwestern Minnesota at an elevation of 1,600 feet, this high plains site endures high winds and below-freezing temperatures in the winter and blistering temperatures (80°F–100°F) in the summer.

Soothe Your Spirit
Stand before the Three Sisters (large boulders) guarding the entrance of the quarry and offer prayers for healing and wholeness. Follow the paved Circle Trail to see Native Americans quarrying the red stone using only hand tools, Winnewissa Falls tumbling over massive boulders, and tall prairie grass swaying in the wind.

A Deeper Look
According to legend, the Great Spirit slaughtered buffalo on the site, turning the ground red, and from that sacred red earth the first human was formed.

Plaza Uta el-Hammam⊕
Chefchaouen, Morocco

I have spent my days stringing and unstringing my instrument while the song I came to sing remains unsung.
—Rabindranath Tagore (1861–1941), Indian writer and Nobel laureate

With fortified walls to protect against medieval invaders, Chefchaouen is tucked safely into the majestic Rif Mountains not far from Tangier. Here, away from the hustle and bustle of the modern world, a pilgrim can take respite in the refuge of the seventeenth-century mosque, sit under the mulberry trees sipping mint tea, or wander beneath the cypress in the castle garden.

If you are ready to put away your smartphone and enjoy some peace and quiet, let your senses be calmed by the sanctuary of Chefchaouen. Daily CTM buses run from Tangier, Fez, Casablanca, Tetouen, Cueta, and Meknes.

Soothe Your Spirit
Notice the sacredness of each moment as you walk along the cobblestone streets and marvel at the soft hues of the sky, horn-shaped mountain peaks, houses awash in shades of blue, and flocks of sheep dotting the landscape. Breathe the mountain air.

A Deeper Look
Despite the bustling trade in marijuana that openly goes on in Chefchaouen, there is practically no crime, and it is one of the safest cities in Morocco. Spanish language is widely spoken here because of the community's proximity to the border with Spain.

Prambanan Temple✳
Central Java, Indonesia

Enlightenment is not imagining figures of light,
but making the darkness conscious.
—Carl Gustav Jung (1875–1961), Swiss psychiatrist

Called the most beautiful Hindu temple in Indonesia, the Prambanan Temple complex actually contains many temples, including three dedicated to the Hindu trinity of Brahma, Vishnu, and Shiva, the Creator, Sustainer, and Destroyer, respectively. With its various lovely temples, astonishing panels of relief depicting the story of the Ramayana, and a magnificent tree of life, the Prambanan Temple stands as a masterpiece of tenth-century sacred Hindu architecture.

If you want to deepen your faith or experience the centuries-old holy temple art, visit Java's Prambanan Temple. The temple is located approximately 11 miles from Yogyakarta.

Allow for a full day to see this temple and arrive early, as crowds of tourists are already arriving at 9:00 a.m. (the temple opens at 6:00 a.m.). The nearest airport, Yogyakarta, is about 6 miles from Prambanan and serves Jakarta, Bali, and Singapore. There is also direct bus service to the temple complex through Trans Jogja, running about every twenty minutes from Malioboro Street in Yogyakarta. Taxis will also take you to the complex. Once you are at the temple, there is a miniature train to take you around if you find the walking too strenuous.

Soothe Your Spirit
Choose a place to meditate, possibly the serene and sheltering temple garden, and, using a one-two-three count for three breaths, intensify and lift your consciousness with each inward breath, attaching to it a Divine name as you breathe out.

A Deeper Look
The complex once held 237 temples in three zones: outer, middle, and inner; the latter is considered the most holy of the three.

Prambanan Temple, Central Java, Indonesia

Puerta de Hayu Marca or Doorway of the Amaru Meru (Gate of the Gods) ⊕
Puno, Peru

The forest is not a resource for us;
it is life itself...the only place for us to live.
—Rigoberta Menchú Tum (1959–), Guatemalan rights activist
for indigenous people and Nobel laureate

Thirty-five miles from Puno, on the shores of sacred Lake Titicaca, juts a mysterious landscape of rock formations that resemble buildings and other structures; sometimes unexplained balls of light appear. But the most puzzling feature of this amazing landscape, known as the "City of the Gods," is the door cut into a massive block of bedrock with a smaller doorway carved into the bottom; local people call it a "gateway to the lands of the gods."

Whether you want to experience higher consciousness through contact with the magnetic energies of ancient holy places or are intrigued by the mysterious sites of ancient civilizations, visit Puerta de Hayu Marca. The nearest airport is Inca Manco Càpac International in nearby Juliaca, but many visitors arrange their trip through Lima. Trains run from Cuzco or Arequipa to Puno, and buses travel daily among the three cities. Contact tour agencies in Puno for a local guide.

Out of respect for the local people, do not take their pictures; they believe photographs pull out their souls.

Soothe Your Spirit
Some people who have knelt in prayer in the ancient doorway feel dizzy or as if they were flying (sensations similar to meditation or a dream), suggestive of transitioning into higher consciousness. If you experience these sensations, declare your intention to manifest larger-than-life dreams of transformation and enlightenment, drawing upon the Inca's sacred wisdom.

A Deeper Look
According to local legends, the great heroes passed through Puerta de Hayu Marca to meet their gods and embrace immortality; in rare instances, they returned with the gods to revisit their kingdom on Earth. This is also called "Spirit Forest" for the strange rock formations that archaeologists believe were carved by an ancient civilization.

Pura Luhur Uluwatu Temple❋
Bali, Indonesia

Of one seldom seen.
—Polynesian proverb

Bali's warm hospitality, Technicolor sunsets, and gorgeous beaches are a few of the many splendors that have earned Indonesia the name "Land of Smiles." Another reason is its spectacular temples, and one of the most amazing and sacred is Pura Luhur Uluwatu. Facing southwest and perched on a cliff more than 200 feet above the Indian Ocean, Uluwatu (as it is known locally) is one of nine directional temples that protect the island from evil spirits. Built in the eleventh century, this Balinese sea temple is made of black coral.

If you yearn for a spiritual island getaway with your lover or your closest friend, travel to Bali and visit Uluwatu Temple. Fly into Bali Ngurah Rai Airport (Denpasar International Airport), 8 miles south of Denpasar in southern Bali. Tours are available, or reach the temple by auto, taxi, or motor scooter.

Soothe Your Spirit
Join with your partner or friends in a meditation or devotional walk, envisioning or praying for a long and joyful relationship. Hold hands and watch the sun set over the Indian Ocean, stretching as far as the eye can see.

A Deeper Look
Every night, locals gather at Uluwatu Temple for kecak and fire communal dances, which begin at sunset and culminate in a ceremonial bonfire.

Pyramid of the Sun—Teotihuacán☯

Mexico City, Mexico

The conscious mind may be compared to a fountain, playing in the sun and falling back into the great subterranean pool of the subconscious from which it rises.
—Sigmund Freud (1856–1939), Austrian psychologist

The Pyramid of the Sun, one of the three largest pyramids in the world, towers 215 feet over the Mexican landscape. A sacred stone monument, according to some theories, it is dedicated to the Great Goddess, one of two main Teotihuacán deities. The cave beneath the pyramid may have been associated with the human emergence (from the "womb") and the clover leaf–shaped chambers off the cave may have been the sacred site of water and fire rituals.

If you want to visit an ancient site to feel its energy, this is it. The nearest airport is in Mexico City. Take a bus from Mexico City's north bus terminal; Autobuses Teotihuacán travel between the site and the town every thirty to sixty minutes, or purchase a coach tour from various tour businesses or hotels in Mexico City.

Soothe Your Spirit

Meditate on top of the pyramid. Imagine warm energy running from your tailbone to the top of your head on the right side of your spine and cool energy returning from the top of your head to your tailbone on the left side. Do several cycles.

A Deeper Look

A second pyramid, the Pyramid of the Moon, is connected to the Pyramid of the Sun by the roughly mile-long Avenue of the Dead. The most visited archaeological sites in Mexico, both were once plastered and painted red and covered in magnificent murals; today only the natural color of the stone remains.

Pyramid of the Sun—Teotihuacán, Mexico City, Mexico

Queen of Peace Shrine
(Shrine of Medjugorje) ◠
Medjugorje, Bosnia and Herzegovina

And a certain man was there, which had an infirmity thirty and eight years. When Jesus saw him...he saith, Rise, take up thy bed, and walk.
—Bible, John 5:5–8

On June 24, 1981, six Croatian children witnessed an apparition of a woman holding a child on a hillside. Although they were afraid, fear did not stop them from returning the next day. Upon seeing the apparition again, they prayed the Rosary. On the third day, the apparition identified herself as the Blessed Virgin. On the fifth day, the children returned with villagers, but only the children could see and hear the lady. On the sixth day, the first of many miraculous healings occurred. Subsequently, a shrine dedicated to the Queen of Peace was erected in the square of the local parish church of Saint James.

Whether you desire a healing miracle or would like to venerate Mary, plan a pilgrimage to Medjugorje. No photos are allowed during worship services and periods of adoration; no lighting of candles is allowed on Apparition Hill and Cross Mountain; and no religious articles can be brought into those sacred sites.

Soothe Your Spirit
Climb Apparition Hill and meditate on holistic wellness. In Saint James Church, light a candle and pray near the wooden cross or attend the evening service when special healing prayers are said.

A Deeper Look
Millions of pilgrims visit the Marian shrine each year; the anniversary of the apparitions is a popular time of pilgrimage.

Rollright Stones⬥
Little Rollright, Oxfordshire, England

Strength of stone, refreshing water, / in peaceful place of green.
Strength of water, fresher flowering, / Peaceful stone has ever been. /
Strength of growth, refreshing stone, / Peace of water to be seen.
—Druid blessing

Nothing epitomizes strength and staying power like stone, and the large upright stones in the little village of Oxfordshire form megaliths—large, upright stone monuments used for religious worship and ritual—dating from 4000 to 2000 B.C. (Neolithic to Bronze Age). The Rollright Stones include three megaliths: the Whispering Knights (the oldest and so named because the stones lean inward), the solitary King Stone, and the King's Men (a circle of stones 104 feet in diameter).

If you long to develop the spiritual strength of a stone or to derive sacred energy from Neolithic ritual sites, journey to the Rollright Stones. Travel to the village of Little Rollright by automobile from Chipping Norton, the nearest town. The site is open daily, sunrise to sunset. There is a small entrance fee. Note that Wyatt's Plant Centre (a mile away) has restrooms and water, as neither are available at the site.

Soothe Your Spirit
Stroll around the Druidical megaliths, absorbing their ancient spiritual energy. Cast a sacred circle of small stones and pray that your faith will always sustain you.

A Deeper Look
The King Stone monolith stands across the road in a different county (Warwickshire) from the King's Men circle.

Rosslyn Chapel
(Collegiate Chapel of Saint Matthew)◓

Roslin, Midlothian, Scotland

The whole value of solitude depends upon oneself; it may be a
sanctuary or a prison...a heaven or a hell as we ourselves make it.
—John Lubbock (1834–1913), English biologist and politician

On a hill above Roslin Glen stands a somber fifteenth-century church, the Collegiate Chapel of Saint Matthew. Rosslyn Chapel, as it is commonly known, was intended as a sanctuary where the church's founder, William Saint Clair, could say Divine Office and restore his soul. That makes the chapel's unusual interior all the more so, for the walls are covered with a strange assortment of ornate carvings, including images of knights, Lucifer, corn (unknown to Europe at that time), and the Green Man, a pagan deity. Famous for its alleged connections with the Knights Templar and the Freemasons, the chapel remains shrouded in mystery. Neither the chapel's riotous carvings nor its dark mysteries disturbed Saint Clair, who relished his sanctuary until his death in 1484.

Whether you wish to find a place of solace or to see this curious sanctuary, you can visit Rosslyn Chapel, south of Roslin. From Edinburgh Airport, travel by bus, rail, taxi, or rental car. No photography or video is allowed inside the chapel.

Soothe Your Spirit
Tour the chapel, making note of images that comfort and unsettle you. Later, use those impressions to create your own sanctuary.

A Deeper Look
Rosslyn Chapel has fueled the imaginations of many artists and writers, including Dan Brown, in whose novel *The Da Vinci Code* the chapel figures largely.

Russian Church of Mary Magdalene❂
Gethsemane, Jerusalem, Israel

Jesus saith unto her, Mary. She turned herself, and saith
unto him, Rabboni; which is to say, Master.
—Bible, John 20:16

Czar Alexander III of Russia's vision of a splendid church honoring his mother, Empress Maria Alexandrovna, named for Saint Mary Magdalene, on the Mount of Olives in Gethsemane (near where Jesus prayed), materialized as this incomparable Russian Orthodox church dedicated to the saint. Built in 1888, the Muscovite-style church is a notable landmark with a dazzling white sandstone facade, a circular blue and gold mosaic iconostasis of Mary Magdalene, a gabled roof adorned in faux lace trim, seven gilded domes crowned with crosses, and glorious sacred art, including the sixteenth-century icon of the Virgin with Child lovingly called Prompt Succor.

If you wish to see incredible sacred artistry or to summon the spiritual steadfastness of Mary Magdalene or the Divine succor of the Holy Mother, visit the Russian Church of Mary Magdalene. Travel to the church by rental car or local public transportation. Visiting hours are 10:00 a.m. to 12:00 p.m., Tuesday and Thursday.

Soothe Your Spirit
As you explore this peaceful sanctuary, feel Mother Mary's nurturing presence and Mary Magdalene's indomitable spirit. Offer a prayer of gratitude for the comfort and support of your faith.

A Deeper Look
The church's crypt contains the relics of the martyred Orthodox saint, the Grand Duchess Elizabeth Feodorovna of Russia, and her niece, Princess Alice of Greece, mother-in-law of Queen Elizabeth II and a rescuer of Jews during the Nazi occupation of Greece.

Saint Catherine's Chapel ◕
Abbotsbury, Dorset, England

A husband, Saint Catherine, / A handsome one, Saint Catherine, /
A rich one, Saint Catherine, / A nice one, Saint Catherine, /
And soon, Saint Catherine.

—Old English prayer

When sailors had to cross Lyme Bay at night to Abbotsbury or worshippers set off to church, they only had to look toward the beacon of the medieval chapel perched on the hill behind the village to find their way. Dedicated to Saint Catherine, the stone chapel has served as a house of worship, a navigational beacon, and a place for women to pray for a husband (to get one or for the safe passage and enduring love of the one they had).

If you would like to pray for the safety and protection of a loved one, come to Saint Catherine's Chapel some summer morning. Abbotsbury sits in southern England, near the west end of the English Channel. Two rail lines connect Dorset County to London, or you can take the B3157 to Abbotsbury, approximately 9 miles west of Weymouth.

Soothe Your Spirit

Walk up the hill from the village to the chapel to pray and then enjoy the views over Lyme Bay, the Fleet (the inlet of water), and Chesil Beach.

A Deeper Look

Saint Catherine's Chapel, according to local lore, may have been spared destruction during the Dissolution of the Monasteries between 1536 and 1541 by King Henry VIII because of its value as a navigational tool.

Saint Catherine's Monastery⊕
Sinai, Egypt

*Now the priest of Midian had seven daughters: and they came
and drew water...And Moses was content to dwell with the man:
and he gave Moses Zipporah his daughter.*
—Bible, Exodus 2:16–21

S aint Catherine's Monastery (also Katherine, in the Orthodox tradition) is
home to one of the world's largest and most precious collections of sacred
manuscripts. Built in A.D. 527, it is one of the oldest Eastern Orthodox religious
communities. Its library holds magnificent paintings, Byzantine icons, sacerdo-
tal ornaments, illuminated manuscripts, and reliquaries. The monastery is situated on the holy site believed to have been where Moses saw the burning bush,
heard God's voice, and (on the mountain above the monastery) received the
Ten Commandments. The fortified compound is named for Saint Catherine,
the Alexandrian Christian martyr whose body, according to legend, was carried away by angels and discovered five centuries later on a nearby mountain
peak (today, a reliquary next to the main altar holds the saint's relics).

 If you seek spiritual uplifting in a sacred sanctuary protected in a fortified
compound, visit the ancient pilgrimage site of Saint Catherine's. Fly from Cairo
to Sharm el-Sheikh, but plan on a three-hour trip to the monastery.

Soothe Your Spirit
Embrace the feeling of protection
provided by the 9-foot-thick walls
that rise 60 feet to protect the
sanctuary and the natural spring
where Moses met his future wife,
Zipporah.

A Deeper Look
Some say the library of Saint
Catherine's Monastery rivals that of
the Vatican.

Saint Catherine's Monastery, Sinai, Egypt

Saint Gabriel Church✚
Kulubi, Ethiopia

Blessed are the merciful, for these shall obtain mercy.
—Bible, Matthew 5:7

When the parishioners of the Orthodox Saint Gabriel Church in Kulubi desire to thank the archangel Gabriel for removing diseases and afflictions from their children, they embark on an end-of-the-year pilgrimage, bringing votive offerings along with spiritual vows and sacred promises. If a baby was born through Gabriel's intervention, parents also bring the infant for baptism. The muscular-looking church on a hill overlooking the dusty plain welcomes Orthodox Christians, Muslims (who call the archangel Gabriel "Jibril," as it is found in the Qur'an), and Animists who revere the sacred site where a tree once stood in place of the church.

If you desire to pray for healing for a child or for someone else, visit Saint Gabriel Church in Kulubi. Come in December when the weather is dry. From Addis Ababa, fly to Dire Dawa or take the overnight train or a daily bus. Minibuses also run from the nearby towns of Harar or Dire Dawa to Kulubi; the latter is roughly 42 miles. Dress appropriately. Bring the gift of a candle or umbrella, the most popular offerings along with livestock.

Soothe Your Spirit
Put on a *gabi* (white cotton shawl that Orthodox Christians in the area wear). Say prayers of thanksgiving for a healing, leaving behind your offering.

A Deeper Look
Kulubi is the largest place of pilgrimage in Ethiopia.

Saint Ives Parish Church⬤
Cornwall, England

*I am sailing into the wind and the dark. I'm doing
my best to keep my boat steady and my sails full.*
—Arthur Ashe (1943–1993), American athlete

Saint Ives Parish Church, in the picturesque seaside town of Saint Ives, Cornwall, on the southwest English coast, is dedicated to three saints: Ia (who, legend has it, crossed the Irish Sea on a cabbage leaf), Andrew (patron of fishermen), and Peter (the Rock). The medieval church of Cornish granite has an 80-foot tower that stands as a spiritual beacon to seamen and parishioners alike, guiding them safely and steadily to the place where heaven, Earth, and the sea meet.

To feel the energy that continuous worship for more than six hundred years has created, visit this sacred sanctuary. The church is located on Saint Andrews Street near the intersection of Highways B3306 and A3074.

Soothe Your Spirit
Feed your spirit by reading stories about the journeys of safe passage by Saint Ia or the apostles Andrew and Peter and enjoy a worship service in this Anglican church.

A Deeper Look
The church was consecrated in 1434. The region of Cornwall is recognized by the Cornish people as one of the Celtic nations, with a cultural identity distinct and different from the rest of England.

Saint Michael's Chapel ⬯

Košice, Slovakia

One joy shatters a hundred griefs.
—Chinese proverb

When the Saint Michael's cemetery chapel, adjacent to the beautiful High Gothic–style Saint Elizabeth's Cathedral in Košice, was undergoing renovation, seventeen gravestones from the fourteenth through the seventeenth centuries were discovered in the chapel's lower level. The headstones were removed and bricked into the exterior. Today, Saint Michael's altar bears the image of the patron saint of the dead—Archangel Michael—as well as the archangels Gabriel and Raphael.

If your spiritual goal is to work through a grieving process because of a catastrophic loss, embark on a trip to Saint Michael's. The nearest airport is Košice International Airport with daily service to Prague and Bratislava. Highway E50 links Košice with Presov. The train station has daily connections to many cities in Slovakia, Poland, and Hungary, including Prague, Bratislava, and Budapest.

Soothe Your Spirit

Reflect on the five stages of grief outlined in the Kübler-Ross model: denial, anger, bargaining, depression, and acceptance. Understand that there is no need to hurry the process. Let this cemetery chapel, now classified as a church, be a loving reminder that death and birth are bookends to a life; this has been true since the birth of humanity.

A Deeper Look

Saint Michael's was built in the center of a cemetery in the heart of the city, and the lower level served as an ossuary (to house bones), while the upper level was used for requiems or services to offer prayers for the deceased.

Saint Patrick's Cathedral☯
New York City, New York, United States

...If two of you agree on earth about anything they ask, it will be done for them by thy Father in heaven. For where two or three are gathered in my name, there am I among them.
—Bible, Matthew 18:29–20

Approaching Saint Patrick's Cathedral on busy Fifth Avenue in Midtown Manhattan, you may be struck by how different it is from the surrounding cityscape. The cathedral appears to be more medieval European than the nineteenth-century New Yorker it is. Built in 1858, Saint Patrick's is a neo-Gothic masterpiece with a lavishly decorated marble facade and many squared spires, including two flanking the grand front entrance and rising 330 feet from street level. You will feel as if you are entering a different world as you step from the bustling city street through the entrance and inside the nave. Cavernous and quiet, this sanctuary surrounds its visitors with peace as the sunlight shimmers through exquisite stained glass windows and reveals soaring arches and stunning artwork. So it is that more than five million faithful and hopeful from around the globe are drawn to Saint Patrick's Cathedral each year.

Whether you seek deeper communion with the universal family or your own family, come to Saint Patrick's Cathedral. Find it in Midtown Manhattan on Fifth Avenue between Fiftieth and Fifty-First streets, six blocks from Grand Central Station (rail), near subway and bus stops, or you can always hail a taxi.

Soothe Your Spirit
Light a candle and pray for a special intention for loved ones.

A Deeper Look
Among the cathedral's extraordinary works of sacred art are two altars by Tiffany & Company, Charles Connick's rose window, and a *Pietà* by William Ordway Partridge that is three times larger than Michelangelo's original.

Saint Peter's Basilica
(Blessed Sacrament Chapel)◕
Rome, Italy

Darkness can only be scattered by light,
hatred can only be conquered by love.
—Pope John Paul II (1920–2005)

When the late Pope John Paul II unexpectedly visited Saint Peter's Basilica—the world's largest church of Christian faith—he purportedly lamented to attendants that it had become more a museum than a church, as there was no place reserved for prayers. The Holy Father apparently thought the basilica's Blessed Sacrament Chapel fit the bill, because he said Mass there, and now signage states that the sanctuary is reserved exclusively for prayer.

The immense chapel features lustrous marble floors, gold-patterned walls, and glorious sacred art. Perhaps the most precious piece is the gilded bronze tabernacle by Bernini, in front of which the Blessed Sacrament is displayed for the "continuous adoration of the faithful." If you seek peaceful haven in a place where Divine art calls the heart to prayer, come to the Blessed Sacrament Chapel. To avoid the crowds, rise early and catch a taxi or take the metro, especially if you want to attend the chapel's 8:30 a.m. Mass.

Soothe Your Spirit
Pray for inspiration about how to express greater selfless love as you reflect upon the meaning of the Blessed Sacrament (the body of Christ sacrificed for the sake of the world).

A Deeper Look
The Eucharist is often given in the Blessed Sacrament Chapel, which has been called the "heart and soul" of Saint Peter's Basilica and the most mystical of its eleven chapels.

Saint Peter's Basilica (Blessed Sacrament Chapel), Rome, Italy

Sainte-Anne-de-Beaupré
Sanctuaire (Shrine)◉
Québec City, Québec, Canada

But I will restore health unto thee, and I will
heal thee of thy wounds, saith the Lord...
—Bible, Jeremiah 30:17

When a fire destroyed the seventeenth-century church dedicated to Saint Anne—the grandmother of Jesus, the mother of the Blessed Virgin Mary, and patroness of the sick—in Québec City in 1922, a magnificent new house of worship was constructed in the shape of a Latin cross. Today, this holy sanctuary features 240 exquisite stained glass windows in the basilica, gorgeous sculpted columns, and a dozen chapels where parishioners and pilgrims flock for worship and prayer. Locals join pilgrims from around the world for the nine-day novena preceding Saint Anne's feast day, July 26, when the sick and infirm come to pray for miraculous cures. There have been many, as any visitor can see by the collection of crutches, bandages, canes, and wheelchairs left behind near the main entrance.

Whether you seek the intercession of Saint Anne for an affliction or would like to venerate the mother of Mary and the grandmother of Jesus, visit this magnificent basilica in the French-speaking city of Québec.

Soothe Your Spirit
Light a candle for yourself or another, kneel, and recite the prayer of the sick.

A Deeper Look
The Redemptorist Order has administered and protected this shrine for 130 years. It attracts more than five hundred thousand pilgrims from all over the world, many seeking healing of body, mind, or spirit.

San Fernando Cathedral☙
San Antonio, Texas, United States

For death is no more than a turning of us over from time to eternity.
—William Penn (1644–1718), Quaker and visionary

The gorgeous focal point of this old Texas cathedral, built in 1738, is an ornate gold tabernacle of the Crucified Christ and the Holy Spirit, surrounded by heart-stopping retablos (devotional paintings based on church art) of saints, believed to have been created in Seville, Spain. A majestic statue of King Ferdinand III of Spain, namesake of the cathedral, appears to stand as guardian and protector of the sanctuary's beautiful treasures: shrines to Our Lady of Candlemas, patroness of the Canary Islands, and Our Lady of Guadalupe, a reliquary containing the relics of the "Heroes of the Alamo," and a coffin engraved with the Lone Star that holds remains of the fallen soldiers.

If your heart is heavy over the loss of a soldier and praying would lighten your spirit, come pray in the San Fernando Cathedral. It is located at 115 Main Plaza, in the downtown area between Highways 10 and 37.

Soothe Your Spirit

Let the grief wash over you. Pray to the Lord and his Holy Mother to help you bear the burden of loss. Give thanks when you feel your heart growing lighter and the weight of grief shifting.

A Deeper Look

It was from the tower of San Fernando that General Antonio Lopez de Santa Ana ordered the dropping of the red flag to start the battle of the Alamo.

Sanchi Stupa (also Sanchi Hill) ✱
Sanchi, Madhya Pradesh, India

Peace comes from within. Do not seek it without.
—Siddhartha Gautama, the Buddha (563–483 B.C.), father of Buddhism

The Great Stupa of Sanchi, built by Emperor Ashoka in the third century B.C., is a large hemispheric dome of mud-colored brick crowned with a *chatra* (resembling a parasol or umbrella) inside a *harmika* (a small platform with a railing). This is the oldest, largest, grandest, and most sacred of several stupas (bell-shaped towers) on Sanchi Hill, which also includes temples, megalithic pillars, and other sacred structures constructed over a period of 1,300 years. Unique to these stupas is that not one bears the image of Lord Buddha; instead, he is represented by carvings of symbolic images such as wheels (teaching) and the lotus (enlightenment).

Whether you seek spiritual insight or assurance, visit Sanchi Stupa, a World Heritage site. The nearest airport (29 miles) is in Bhopal; the nearest rail station (6.5 miles) is in Vidisha. From Bhopal, Vidisha, or Indore, you can travel to Sanchi by taxi, rental car, bus, or auto rickshaw.

Soothe Your Spirit
Circumambulate the Great Stupa, mindful that you are moving ever closer to your spiritual solar plexus: the source of Divine "gut" messages. At the center, stand or sit in lotus position in zazen (quiet meditation) to receive the whisper of wisdom or succor you seek.

A Deeper Look
In the Vihara (Buddhist monastery) on Sanchi Hill, a glass chest enshrines the holy relics of Buddha, which originally were interred in the Great Stupa.

Sanjusangendo Hall✱
Kyoto, Japan

The secret of existence is to have no fear.
—Siddhartha Gautama, the Buddha (563–483 B.C.), father of Buddhism

This twelfth-century Heian temple with vermilion columns, emerald roof, and serene gardens epitomizes Japanese court life in this bustling city from A.D. 794 to 1869. The spacious terrace offers stunning vistas of Sanjusangendo Hall with its 6-foot-tall statue of Kannon, goddess of mercy, who has eleven faces and a thousand arms. Flanking the large statue are 1,001 smaller Kannons, each having forty arms that each have the power to save twenty-five worlds.

If you desire to be a force of good in the world, visit Sanjusangendo Temple. Located in the Higashiyama District of Kyoto, the temple is open 8:00 a.m. to 5:00 p.m. in summer, 9:00 a.m. to 4:00 p.m. in winter (November to March). From the Kyoto train station, Sanjusangendo is a fifteen- to twenty-minute walk; you can also take a city bus. No photography is allowed within the temple.

Soothe Your Spirit

In the hall of the Kannons, drop some money in a donation box, then strike the gong three times and say a prayer for the courage and conviction to do God's work. Light three sticks of incense: for the Buddha (the Divine one), the dharma (the law and discipline that guides one's life), and the sangha (the community).

A Deeper Look

The hall housing the Kannons is made in the Wayo Japanese style, long and large enough to house the statues and allow thirty-three spaces (a number sacred to Buddha) between the columns.

Santiago de Compostela Cathedral (Shrine of Saint James)⬣
Santiago de Compostela, Spain

...The Lord is full of compassion and mercy.
—Bible, James 5:11

After the bones of the apostle James, one of three to witness Jesus' Transfiguration, were discovered in northwestern Spain, a chapel was built to safeguard the relics. Centuries later, Santiago de Compostela Cathedral was built on the site. This magnificent basilica, constructed in the style of the Latin cross, features soaring vaulted arches and a central window through which holy light seems to bathe visitors.

Catch a bus or taxi from either of two international airports, but get an early start as throngs of pilgrims soon fill this World Heritage site. When entering through the cathedral's carved Pórtico de la Gloria, notice the carving of James on the central pillar; a groove has been worn in the stone where pilgrims have been touching it in prayer since the twelfth century.

Soothe Your Spirit
Place your fingers in the grooves of the Tree of Jesse on the central pillar topped with a statue of Saint James seated. Pray that your heart might be opened to Saint James's messages of love.

A Deeper Look
Santiago de Compostela, the third holiest city in Christendom (after Jerusalem and Rome), hosts a massive celebration each year on July 25, the feast day of James, Spain's patron saint.

Santiago de Compostela Cathedral (Shrine of Saint James), Santiago de Compostela, Spain

Sheela Na Gig (Kilpeck Church)◉
Hereford, Herefordshire County, England

If facts are the seeds which later produce knowledge and wisdom,
then the emotions and the impressions of the senses
are the fertile soil in which seeds must grow.
—Rachel Carson (1907–1964), marine biologist and ecological writer

Sheela Na Gig, viewed alternatively as a plumpish and sensual goddess or a thin and menacing hag, always exhibits an exaggerated vulva—a surprise for many people who do not expect such exhibitionist art on a church. However, Sheela Na Gig is associated with childbirth and is a medieval embellishment on many churches throughout England and Ireland. The Kilpeck Church (formerly the parish church of Saints Mary and David in Kilpeck), which sits in the English countryside bordering Wales, has some of the country's most notable Romanesque adornment, dating from 1140, including a well-preserved carving of Sheela Na Gig among the corbels of the apse.

If you are interested in Celtic ideas of fertility, come to Kilpeck village to visit this Anglican church. It's located about 8 miles southwest of Hereford in Herefordshire County.

Soothe Your Spirit
Soak up the peace and quiet in this lovely little church in the most rural county in England, and then walk around outside. Open your creative mind to the fecundity that surrounds you: sketch images, jot notes, read about Celtic beliefs, and see what develops.

A Deeper Look
Many of the church's Romanesque carvings feature sacred images of nature, including a tree of life carved on the south door tympanum.

Shiprock⊘
Navajo Nation, New Mexico, United States

Be still and the earth will speak to you.

—Navajo proverb

The forty-million-year-old volcanic Shiprock Peak, rising out of the high desert floor to an elevation of 1,800 feet, may look like a nineteenth-century ship to outsiders, but to the Navajo it looks like a winged rock. In fact, according to legend, *Tsé Bit'a'í* (as it is called by the Navajo) was once the dwelling place of a mythological great bird that carried the tribe's ancestors from their home in the north to their new home in the southwest. Another of the many myths associated with *Tsé Bit'a'í* is that it is a medicine pouch carried by a powerful mountain spirit.

If you would like to experience the Navajo healing ceremony known as Ye-ibichai (Night Way), visit Shiprock. It lies at the intersection of Highways 64 and 491, with the nearest towns being Cortez, Colorado, and Farmington, New Mexico.

Soothe Your Spirit

Find a guide willing to help you understand the portions of the ceremony you are allowed to see. Feel the healing energy of the chanting. Create a self-healing chant (for example, "My body is in the process of returning to perfection: every cell, every organ, every system").

A Deeper Look

Shiprock, in the Four Corners region, is the site of the Navajo Nation's annual October festival, which includes a nine-day healing ceremony. Photographs and videos of the sacred ceremony are prohibited, as are hiking and climbing on the sacred peak.

Shrine of Our Lady of Montserrat ◉
Basilica of Montserrat Monastery, Catalonia, Spain

Draw nigh to God and he will draw nigh to you.
—Bible, James 4:8

The *Black Madonna (La Moreneta) and Child* is a sacred sculpture in the Monastery of Montserrat that, according to a legend, was carved by Saint Luke and brought to Spain where it was hidden from the Moors until the ninth century A.D. when it was discovered on the mountain of Montserrat. A monastery was established there, and today a magnificent basilica enshrines the miracle-producing icon that draws millions of pilgrims each year.

If you have felt spiritually estranged from the faith (in which you were raised or once embraced), start the process of reconciliation with a visit to the monastery to see the Black Madonna. The monks welcome visitors to their sacred sanctuary located near the summit of the 4,000-foot mountain. The best way to get there is to fly to Barcelona and take a taxi to Plaça d'Espanya. Once there, catch one of a dozen trains to Montserrat that connect with an aerial lift to reach the monastery.

Soothe Your Spirit
Participate in a Mass or recitation of the Liturgy of the Hours and start reconnecting your heart with the Divine within who has never left you.

A Deeper Look
The Black Madonna's color is probably due to the passage of time and smoke from devotional candles and varnishes.

Shrine of Rumi⊗
Konya, Turkey

This is love: to fly toward a secret sky, to cause a hundred veils to fall each moment. First to let go of life. Finally, to take a step without feet.
—Jalal al-Din Rumi (1207–1273), Persian poet and mystic

The Sufi poet Rumi was so absorbed with his love for the Divine that he danced through the streets of medieval Konya, praying and whirling in ecstasy. Today, in the heart of this conservative city located three hours (by car) south of Ankara, the turquoise dome of Rumi's mausoleum rises rapturously toward the heavens, and its ornate interior pulsates with ethereal beauty, while, over the city's din, the muezzin calls out *adhān* (call to prayer).

Whether you yearn to deepen your love for the Divine or to see Rumi's resting place, the Green Dome, now known as the Mevlâna Museum, is a sight to behold. The mausoleum's towering walls, adorned with enameled reliefs and Islamic script, encircle the gold-draped tomb of Mevlâna (Our Guide), as Rumi is called by the Whirling Dervish sect he inspired. An adjoining room displays ancient manuscripts, prayer beads, musical instruments, and other artifacts.

Soothe Your Spirit
Read Rumi's poetry and reflect on the twirling meditation that Rumi practiced to empty himself of ego in order to dwell on thoughts of the Divine. Feel your footsteps grow lighter as devotional love fills your heart.

A Deeper Look
Thousands of Muslims and non-Muslims visit the Green Dome annually, many on December 17, the anniversary of Rumi's death— his "wedding night with God." Islam followers place their foreheads on and kiss the silver step of Rumi's shrine.

Sri Ranganathaswamy Temple✲
Srirangam, Trichy, Tamil Nadu, India

*Lead me from the unreal to the Real...from darkness unto Light...
from death to Immortality.*
—Gayatri Mantra

One of the largest Hindu temple complexes in the world is dedicated to Lord Ranganatha, a reclining form of the Hindu deity Vishnu, sustainer of the universe. The stone carvings, bas-reliefs (or carved images that are slightly raised from the surface from which they are carved), and friezes, the horizontal bands that run across doorways and windows, adorn, embellish, and dramatize this colorful temple.

Whether you seek a spiritual awakening or transcendental states of consciousness, or love sacred Indian temple architecture, visit this two-thousand-year-old temple where devotees believe that the Lord is ever-present. It is situated on Srirangam Island in the Kavery River, roughly 10.5 miles north of Trichy, and less than a mile from the Rangam railway station. The nearest airport is in Bangalore. Buses are available from major Indian cities; take a taxi or rental car, purchase a coach tour, or hire a car and driver from one of the hotels.

Come during the dry season (October through May), but start by 7:00 a.m. to avoid the crowds and the heat. Guides are available at the shoe depository. Photography is prohibited.

Soothe Your Spirit
Buy a flower, remove your shoes, and perform a namaskar (bow with hands folded in prayer) before the deity. Sit in meditation, inviting Divine inspiration to fill and sustain you. If you are a non-Hindu, visit the temple as a tourist; incorporate regular periods of silence in your spiritual practice; meditate on God as the Sustainer of All.

A Deeper Look
Millions of Hindus visit each year. The complex encompasses 156 acres and is the holy site of the enlightenment of Ramanujacharya, a preeminent Vaishnava scholar.

Sri Senpaga Vinayagar Temple✲
Singapore

Bountiful guardians of the world...when we
long to win, may we be victors.
—Rig Veda, Book V, Hymn 62:9

If you arrive early enough at this lovely temple dedicated to Ganesh, the elephant-headed god of success, also known as Remover of Obstacles in the Hindu pantheon, you might see the priests ritually preparing the altar and statues for the morning worship (puja). Using jars of water poured amid clouds of incense, the priests intone verses in Sanskrit and ring a bell while washing, drying, and then adorning the idols with brightly colored flowers.

If you seek Divine assistance in attracting success or removing obstacles to create a new beginning, come to Sri Senpaga Vinayagar Temple to pay your respects to Ganesh (also, Ganesha or Ganapati). The temple is in the Tanjong Katong area, twenty minutes from the airport and easily reached by taxi or rental car. No shoes or socks are allowed inside the temple.

Soothe Your Spirit

Offer a flower and ring the bell (if one is provided for devotees) as an invocation to the Divine. In a silent mantra, call his name, *"Aum Shri Ganeshaya Namah"* ("Praise to Lord Ganesha") and ask his assistance in clearing obstacles from within or without and in manifesting spiritual or material abundance.

A Deeper Look

The temple, the second oldest in Singapore, was originally created in the 1850s by the Ceylon Tamils in the ancient south Indian ornate and intricately carved Chola style of architecture but has been reconstructed several times.

Stonehenge⬥
Amesbury, Wiltshire County, England

*Pile of Stone-henge! So proud to hint yet keep / Thy secrets,
thou lov'st to stand and hear / The plain resounding to the
whirlwind's sweep / Inmate of lonesome Nature's endless year.*
—William Wordsworth (1770–1850), English poet

S tonehenge's massive megalithic pillars and lintels, dating to 3200 B.C., were
likely assembled for the purpose of worship. Today, this prehistoric monument in the quiet English countryside on the Salisbury Plain near Amesbury is a
sacred destination for neo-Druids, pagan and neopagan worshippers, and New
Age believers. Many come for summer solstice (June in the Northern Hemisphere), purportedly the most auspicious time for manifesting desires. At dawn
on that day, the sunlight rises above the horizon, cuts across Stonehenge, and
illuminates the pillars and field upon which thousands of believers gather. On
winter solstice, the sun sets between the two biggest megaliths.

If you'd like to experience a magical summer or winter solstice or summon
the magic of fertility or abundance, journey to Stonehenge.

Soothe Your Spirit
Bring an object symbolizing what you
desire. Stand facing the sun in sight
of the megaliths, holding the object
in the open palms of your hands.
Offer thanks to the Divine Source of
All for the blessings in your life. Then
pray for the magic you desire.

A Deeper Look
Some legends claim Stonehenge
was built by King Arthur and Merlin,
others point to the Druids, Danes,
Saxons, Greeks, Romans, Atlanteans,
even the Egyptians.

Stonehenge, Amesbury, Wiltshire County, England

Sultan Ahmed Mosque (Blue Mosque)✪
Istanbul, Turkey

In hardship I saw him on my side.
In ease and well-being I beheld only God.
—from *Rābi'a the Mystic* by Baba Kuhi of Shiraz, ninth-century A.D. Iranian Sufi
poet-saint, trans. Aneela Khalid Arshed

Named for the blue tiles covering the interior walls of the sanctuary, the Blue Mosque was built between A.D. 1609 and 1616 and is a grand representation of Byzantine and Ottoman religious architecture. The commanding mosque is framed by six tall, graceful minarets and surrounded by expansive courtyards. A massive circular chandelier illumines the cavernous domed interior, with its many smaller domes cascading from the main dome, and Arabic calligraphy and floral and geometric motifs embellish the ceilings.

Whether you seek the power of knowledge or spiritual recharging, travel to the Blue Mosque. Remove your shoes before entering. Women must cover their hair with scarves, and if not attired conservatively enough, don robes (available onsite at no charge). Nonworshippers must use the north entrance and are not allowed in during prayer times. Get to the mosque via taxi, tram, or bus to Sultanahmet, Istanbul's tourist area.

Soothe Your Spirit
Fill the gaps in your spiritual knowledge by writing a question or two to ask one of the imams who lead the prayers and preach the sermon on Fridays. Be respectful; this is a holy place of worship.

A Deeper Look
The original seventeenth-century Venetian stained glass windows have been replaced with replicas but still offer a lovely luminosity.

Swaminarayan Akshardham Temple✺
Delhi, India

Still your mind in me, still yourself in me,
and without a doubt you shall be united with me,
Lord of Love, dwelling in your heart.
—Bhagavad Gita

The magnificent Akshardham Temple on the banks of the Yamuna River incorporates pink stone symbolizing bhakti (eternal love) with pure white marble symbolizing peace. Built in 2005, the world's largest Hindu temple is completely covered with ornate carvings and filled to the hilt with artwork. With its fantastic dioramas, IMAX theater, indoor boat ride, numerous exhibits, lighted musical fountain, twenty thousand sculptures of statues and deities, and 60 acres of lawns and gardens, Swaminarayan Akshardham might best be described as a spiritual amusement park.

Visit this temple to seek knowledge about the great spiritual traditions of India, including *prema* (elevated love) and bhakti yoga (the path of love). Allow roughly four hours to see everything. Indira Gandhi International is the nearest airport; from there, taxis, metro trains, city buses, and auto rickshaws (bargain fare) make travel to the temple easy. No cameras, bags, backpacks, food, or water are allowed inside.

Soothe Your Spirit
Behold love for the Divine as you experience the temple and its offerings. Then during meditation, feel the depth and bliss of love in union with the Divine.

A Deeper Look
Thousands of volunteers and seven thousand sculptors worked to complete the temple in five years. With its sublime messages of spiritual love and national pride, Akshardham is a popular tourist attraction for Indians as well as spiritual seekers.

Taj Mahal✴

Agra, India

Only let this one teardrop, this Taj Mahal, glisten
spotlessly bright on the cheek of time, forever and ever.
—Rabindranath Tagore (1861–1941), Indian writer and Nobel laureate

When his beloved wife died giving birth to their fourteenth child in 1631, Shah Jahan spent the next twenty-two years building a suitable resting place for her: the incomparable Taj Mahal (Crown Palace). Often called the most graceful structure on Earth, this shrine to enduring love towers above the banks of the Yamuna River; its white marble dome and twin minarets shimmer in symmetrical perfection, as its mirror image reflects in the gazing pool below.

Whether you are mourning a lost love, celebrating a new one, or still searching, visit the Taj Mahal. Catch an early train from New Delhi or arrive in Agra the night before. Sunrise at this World Heritage site is spectacular.

Remove your shoes to enter the central chamber of the mausoleum, where the light streams through the intricate latticework. Mumtaz's cenotaph, bearing ninety-nine names of Allah, sits in the center of the semiprecious stone–encrusted interior; her husband's modest cenotaph is nearby.

Soothe Your Spirit

Sit by the gazing pool of the Taj Mahal or find another peaceful body of water closer to home. Offer a prayer of love for a loss in your life. Give yourself permission to mourn but also to feel peace.

A Deeper Look

The cenotaphs are only decorative representations of the actual coffins of the shah and his wife, contained in the lower crypt, where the humid air is heavily scented with incense and rose petals.

Taos Pueblo☯

Taos, New Mexico, United States

*Hold on to what is good even if it is a handful of earth. / Hold on
to what you believe, even if it is a tree that stands by itself...*
—Pueblo prayer

Taos Pueblo is the largest red-adobe pueblo (village) in North America—
and one of the few continually occupied since its construction, one
thousand years ago. Despite four centuries of European-American invasion
and influence, the Tuah-Tah (Place of Red Willows) tribe of Pueblo people has
held fast to this stunning structure and to their ancestral (and closely guarded)
traditions.

To gain a new appreciation for the courageous spirit of the Tuah-Tah or to
bolster your own spirit, visit the Taos Pueblo, one of the Eight Northern Pueblos. Drive or fly to Taos, an artistic mecca in northwestern New Mexico, which
is only a few miles from the Pueblo, or take a day trip from Albuquerque or
Santa Fe. Coach tours are available.

The site is open 8:00 a.m. to 4:30 p.m. Monday through Saturday and 8:30
a.m. to 4:30 p.m. on Sundays, except for Pueblo holidays. Honor the visitors
guidelines: www.indianpueblo.org/19-pueblos/visiting-a-pueblo/.

Soothe Your Spirit

Tour the ancient pueblo with respect
while contemplating the resilience
of the Taos people. Write a prayer to
the Great Spirit asking for strength
to hold fast to your spiritual truth.
When you return home, bury the
note beneath a flowering plum, king
protea, or borage; all three plants
symbolize courage.

A Deeper Look

Taos Pueblo is a National Historic
Landmark and a World Heritage
site. In 1970, the United States
government returned 48,000 acres
of sacred mountains and forests that
included Blue Lake, a most sacred
site to the Taos people.

Taos Pueblo, Taos, New Mexico, United States

Temple Church●
London, England

I will lift up mine eyes unto the hills, from whence cometh my help.
—Bible, Psalm 121:1

Founded by the Knights Templar, the order of monks who provided safe passage to pilgrims during the Crusades as they traveled to and from the Holy Land, the Temple Church's round nave finds resonance with the Crusaders' holiest shrine, the Church of the Holy Sepulchre in Jerusalem. Nine marble effigies of medieval knights are placed on the floor of the round nave. The church's spectacular stained glass windows, exquisite altar inscribed with the Ten Commandments, and interior gargoyles made it a stunning setting for scenes from *The Da Vinci Code*.

If you want to pray for your safety or that of someone you love, visit Temple Church, located at Inner Temple Lane, King's Bench Walk. The church is located in a historical area of London between the River Thames and Fleet Street.

Soothe Your Spirit
Read Psalm 121 from the Old Testament about the safety that comes from the Divine in time of human need. Ask God for what you need and give thanks.

A Deeper Look
In 1185, the patriarch of Jerusalem consecrated the round church, designed to symbolize Jerusalem's Church of the Holy Sepulchre.

Temple Emanu-El●

New York City, New York, United States

It is written, "Love the Lord your God and serve
Him with all your heart."
—Bible, Deuteronomy 11:3

Temple Emanu-El is the world's largest Reform Jewish synagogue, accommodating 2,500 worshippers inside the Moorish and art deco interior embellished with handsome mosaics. The exterior limestone walls with Romanesque Revival detailing suggest a building from the medieval period rather than one built in 1928 to serve a growing progressive-minded community that had also assimilated Conservative Jews from Eastern Europe (in the 1930s)—a blending of new, old, West, and East. Today, the "spirit of the congregation" is one of "inclusion, flexibility, and sensitivity to the needs and desires" of worshippers.

If you seek a place that can lift your heart and help you find meaning or would enjoy attending a service in a beautiful, welcoming synagogue, visit Temple Emanu-El. It is located at One East Sixty-Fifth Street, in New York City's Upper East Side, across from Central Park, an easy walk from several subway trains and bus lines.

Soothe Your Spirit

Attend a service and experience the power of prayer embraced by this congregation. Perform a traditional ritual or one of your own urging, as allowed and encouraged here.

A Deeper Look

The Temple Emanu-El complex includes the smaller Beth-El Chapel, a six-story religious school. The temple also has a world-class collection of Judaic art that provides spiritual succor through its aesthetic, social, and religious context.

Temple of Aphrodite❂
Geyre, Turkey

One word frees us of all the weight and pain of life: that word is love.
—Sophocles (496–406 B.C.), Greek playwright and priest

In the Aegean region of Turkey, about an hour and a half from the thermal springs of Pamukkale, sit the sprawling ruins of the ancient city of Aphrodisias, with a temple honoring Aphrodite, goddess of love, at its center. A marble statue of the goddess, recovered from the site, is now displayed in an outstanding museum there. Aphrodite appears in a long garment whose folds contain carved reliefs of the Three Graces with Aphrodite, three cupids with Aphrodite, and the sun god and moon goddess.

If meditating at a temple dating back centuries before Christ and honoring the goddess of love might help you to reconnect with Divine love, visit Aphrodite's Temple. Take a guided tour (the easiest route), or travel by bus or car from Denizli toward Nazilli on to Karacasu and Geyre. See the following website for more information: www.turkeytravelplanner.com/go/Aegean/aphrodisias/trans.html.

Soothe Your Spirit
Rub rose oil (the rose was believed sacred to Aphrodite) into the palm of your right hand, place your hand over your heart, and meditate on God's everlasting love or on your romantic love.

A Deeper Look
Considered a sacred site for six thousand years, Aphrodisias was founded in the third century B.C. and abandoned in the thirteenth century. The Temple of Aphrodite was converted into a Catholic basilica during the Byzantine era and destroyed in the twelfth century.

Temple of Apollo◑
Delphi, Greece

I am in you and you in me, mutual in divine love.
—William Blake, English poet and mystic

B efore Apollo, the sun god of light, could establish the Oracle of Delphi, he first had to defeat the python that guarded the spring. Apparently, that was handily accomplished, because the Temple of Apollo and the Oracle of Delphi became the most sacred sites in the ancient world. People of all classes and ranks undertook the pilgrimage to Delphi (which some believe to be the center of the world) to ask the Oracle for advice and guidance.

If you feel as though you've lost your inner compass, come to Delphi to reset it. The nearest international airport is in Athens; the Temple of Apollo and Oracle of Delphi are in central Greece. The easiest way to see the sight is with a tour. Alternatively, you could rent a car or hire a car and guide to show you around this sacred site.

Soothe Your Spirit

As you stroll, let your mind and body slow to the pace of the ancients, whose only timepiece was the sun. When you feel calm, ask for Divine counsel and wait for a reply from your intuition.

A Deeper Look

A priestess known as the Pythia was the only person allowed to enter the *adytum*, a sacred chamber where the Oracle was given.

Temple of Artemis✷
Ephesus, Turkey

I have seen the walls and Hanging Gardens of ancient Babylon, the statue of Olympian Zeus, the Colossus of Rhodes, the mighty work of the high Pyramids, and the tomb of Mausolus. But when I saw the temple at Ephesus rising to the clouds, all these other wonders were put in the shade.
—Philon of Byzantium (ca. 280–220 B.C.), Greek engineer and writer

On a marshy strip of river land near Ephesus stands a single column and a few fragments of a magnificent ancient temple honoring the Ephesian Artemis, goddess of fertility (also known as Diana, she is not the same as the Greek Artemis, who was goddess of the hunt). The marble temple was once the mother of all monuments, eclipsing even the Parthenon in Athens, testifying to the importance of this goddess of fertility. In fact, the temple was one of the Seven Wonders of the Ancient World.

Whether you wish to attract abundance or a grateful spirit, visit this temple at Ephesus, 2 miles from Selçuk. Go early to avoid the midday heat and tourists. The nearest ship harbor is Kusadasi, and the nearest airport is in nearby Izmir.

Soothe Your Spirit
Chant an affirmation of your desired fertility (whether it is to conceive a child, spawn income streams, or adopt new spiritual insight). Drink a sacrament of pomegranate juice to Artemis of Ephesus.

A Deeper Look
Pomegranate-shaped breasts (or eggs) cover the entire torso of the Ephesian Artemis. According to the Qur'an, pomegranates grow in the gardens of paradise and symbolize God's gifts to humankind.

Temple of Demeter⬟

Sangri, Naxos Island, Greece

Take full account of the excellencies which you possess, and in gratitude remember how you would hanker after them, if you had them not.
—Marcus Aurelius (A.D. 121–180), Roman soldier

Arising from the fertile fields of Naxos in the Cyclades chain of Greek Islands is the partially reconstructed Temple of Demeter, whom the ancients worshipped as goddess of fecundity and grain. Several important and secretive rituals were associated with Demeter, including one performed in autumn to promote a good harvest. However, the most famous rituals to Demeter were the Eleusinian Mysteries, in which the worshipper petitioned for "prosperity before death."

If you believe the fecund energy that is said to permeate the ruins of Demeter's temple might increase the productivity of your spiritual life or other endeavors, come to Greece. Once on the island, the best way to get to the temple is by rental car or car and driver. Start from Hora, drive to Filoti, and follow the signs.

Soothe Your Spirit

Enjoy an hour of downtime in the open air, walking around or sitting and gazing at the temple. If no one else is around, take time to meditate, and once your mind is calm, ask for inspiration to start flowing. Record your ideas in a notebook.

A Deeper Look

This temple, unlike many of its ancient counterparts, has a square-shaped floor. A portion of the floor, a wall, columns, and a doorway give an idea of the splendid white stone temple built in the sixth century B.C.

Temple of Demeter, Sangri, Naxos Island, Greece

Temple of Heaven
(literally, Altar of Heaven) ✪
Beijing, China

Heaven means to be one with God.
—Confucius (551–479 B.C.), Chinese philosopher and teacher

When fifteenth-century Chinese emperors wanted to thank the gods for abundance, they journeyed to the Temple of Heaven to offer sacrifices upon the three-tiered Circular Mound Altar and prayers in the trilevel Hall of Prayer for Good Harvest. Just beyond the Imperial Vault of Heaven is Echo Wall, with acoustical properties that allow a whisper spoken at one end to be heard at the other end. The Triple Echo Stones in the courtyard have similar properties; the number of echoes (one, two, or three) depends on where the speaker is standing.

If you feel called to offer prayers of gratitude in a stunning representation of Chinese temple architecture, visit this ancient Taoist temple, built around 1420. Beijing Capital International Airport is about 10.5 miles from the city. From Beijing, take the subway, a taxi, or a city bus. The complex is open year-round, but book a tour in advance because this World Heritage site is one of the most-visited sacred places in Beijing. Allow two hours to see everything.

Soothe Your Spirit
Before or after touring the temple, take a leisurely stroll through the courtyard and gardens. Return the generous smiles of passersby with a smile of gratitude, and then bow your head in respect for this holy place venerating Divine abundance.

A Deeper Look
The Imperial Vault and Hall of Prayer are connected by the Vermilion Steps Bridge (Sacred Way).

Temple of Hera (Heraion)●
Olympia, Athens, Greece

We learn by practice...One becomes in some area an athlete of God.
—Martha Graham (1894–1991), American ballerina and choreographer

The Temple of Hera in Olympia, one of the earliest Greek temples with Doric columns, honored both Hera and Zeus (wife and husband supreme deities) until the Great Temple of Zeus was completed, after which only women worshipped at Hera's temple. Today, the temple is the site where eleven women (representing the Vestal Virgins) ignite the Olympic Torch with the sun's rays, in a ceremony that signals the opening of the Olympic Games. The games are a testament of athletic excellence as well as of respect and cooperation among athletes and countries of the world.

If you seek the focus and dedication of an Olympic athlete in your spiritual life or in your personal relationships, visit the Temple of Hera. From Athens International Airport, travel by bus or train to Olympia.

Soothe Your Spirit

Energize your body and your spirit with a devotional walk amid the sacred ruins of ancient Olympia. At Hera's temple, pause to absorb the heartfelt energy that ancient athletes poured out in prayer and supplication to the deity.

A Deeper Look

The Temple of Hera (ca. 590 B.C.) was among several temples as well as altars, statues, treasuries, and other structures in the Altis (sanctuary, or sacred precinct) of Olympia. The Altis originally included the Olympic Stadium, where people watched the competitions from the Hill of Kronos, but the arena was gradually moved east to its present location.

Temple of Isis⬢
Delos, Greece

If virtue precede us, every step will be safe.
—Seneca (5 B.C.–A.D. 65), Roman dramatist, philosopher, and politician

Ruins are all that remain of the gorgeous Doric-style temple built in Isis's honor by the people of Delos so that fishermen, seafarers, and locals could pray to her for safe passage, protection, good health, and fortune. The temple is flanked by a craggy outcropping and perched stalwartly on a hill that overlooks the harbor of Delos, which is said to be the birthplace of the sun god Apollo and his twin sister, Artemis.

If you have been feeling lost, buffeted by the winds of uncertainty, and you long for a feeling of safe harbor and security, head to Delos and the Temple of Isis. Since there are no overnight accommodations for tourists on Delos, book a day trip on one of the many boats leaving the Mykonos Port.

Soothe Your Spirit
Soak up the light and the subtle energy of the ruins, contemplating your life and how you might achieve a sense of stability and security in the ever-changing world. Consider the possibility of establishing more routines or finding ways to ground yourself through yoga or some other discipline.

A Deeper Look
This small, sacred, desolate island was once the holiest island in all of Greece, and it was even forbidden for anyone to be born or die on the island, as it was the birthplace of gods.

Temple of Isis⊕
Philae, Nubia, Egypt

A grateful mind is a great mind which eventually attracts to itself great things.
—Plato (429–347 B.C.), Greek philosopher and mathematician

The ancient Egyptians built a stunning temple for Isis (wife of Osiris) on the holy island of Philae in the middle of the Nile River, where they worshipped her as goddess of motherhood, magic, fertility, children, and protector of the dead. Recently, the temple had to be moved due to yearly flooding, so the temple complex was deconstructed and painstakingly transferred to another island, where it was reconstructed and the island was renamed Philae.

If you seek fertility of spirit or body and believe that being in the Temple of Isis might benefit your aspirations, visit this site. From Aswan, take the road 4 miles south to a boat landing and then hire a boat to take you to the island. There is an entrance fee to tour the temple and to see the sound and light show.

Soothe Your Spirit

Take as much time as you need to absorb the magical energy of the temple. As you walk, think about how you might attract or manifest the blessing of fertility in your life. When you are ready to leave the site, offer a heartfelt spiritual thank-you to this ancient goddess for any inspiration that came to you during the visit.

A Deeper Look

The towering walls of the temple are covered top to bottom with intricate reliefs depicting scriptural stories sculpted into the stone walls and painted in now fading but once brilliant colors.

Temple of Tellus✚
Dougga, Tunisia

Our duty, as men and women, is to proceed as if limits to our
ability did not exist. We are collaborators in creation.
—Pierre Teilhard de Chardin (1881–1955), French philosopher and Jesuit priest

The Tunisian temple honoring Tellus (also Terra Mater), ancient Roman goddess of marriage (and fertility when coupled with Ceres), survives as part of a well-preserved third-century A.D. Roman town in northern Tunisia. The arid climate of Dougga, believed to have originally been a Berber village, preserves stunning pagan temples, baths, arches, theaters, cisterns, a forum, a market, and a mausoleum.

If you are drawn to the Earth Mother Goddess or to other cults predating the Judeo-Christian era and/or would like to pray in an ancient place of great spiritual and historical significance, visit Dougga. Take a day tour from Tunis or El Kef; hire a taxi from the nearest town, Teboursouk; take the bus from El Kef, disembarking at the Nouvelle Dougga stop and walking 2.5 miles to the temple.

Soothe Your Spirit

Explore the ruins, stopping to meditate before the capitol dedicated to Juno, Roman goddess who protected pregnant women and fetuses, delivering them into the light. Pray for fertility of mind, body, or spirit—for yourself, a loved one, or our leaders, for our earthly home needs solutions to its many problems in order to prevent our civilization from falling as did the Romans.

A Deeper Look

Dougga's capitol, dedicated to three Roman deities—Jupiter, Juno, and Minerva—was built in A.D. 166, and its walls (about 33 feet high) still support the breathtaking portico, where you can stand and look out over the vast desert landscape to blue-purple mountains rising far in the distance.

Temple of Tellus, Dougga, Tunisia

Temple Square (Mormon Temple)◐
Salt Lake City, Utah, United States

The church exists to exalt the family.
And the family is the fundamental unit of the church.
—Russell M. Nelson (1924–), American physician and president
of The Church of Jesus Christ of Latter-day Saints

It is no wonder Temple Square—world headquarters of The Church of Jesus Christ of Latter-day Saints—receives millions of visitors each year. The 10-acre complex is beautiful and welcoming, and it features a dozen historical and sacred sites. Among those open to the public are Assembly Hall (a lovely Gothic church with exquisite stained glass windows); Mormon Tabernacle (a dome-shaped auditorium, where the famed Mormon Tabernacle Choir performs); Joseph Smith Memorial Building (the location of the Family Search Center); and Family History Library (huge repository of genealogy records). The most sacred site—Salt Lake Temple, the "House of the Lord"—is not open to the public, but it is a glory to behold.

Whether you yearn to connect with your ancestral family or to deepen your connection to your church family, try visiting Temple Square in downtown Salt Lake City. Take a shuttle, rental car, taxi, or bus from Salt Lake City International Airport. The visitors center at Temple Square has information on guided tours, shuttles within the complex, guidebooks, concerts, and more.

Soothe Your Spirit
Explore the site that calls to you. Enjoy a concert or a quiet meal with your family. Gaze at the sacred temple (lit like the North Star at night), and pray for help in finding, healing, or strengthening your family.

A Deeper Look
The Humanitarian Center is open to the public and provides resources to help strengthen families.

Temples at Khajuraho✳

Khajuraho, Madhya Pradesh, India

*The Plain is endless space expressed; / Vast is the sky above, /
I only feel, against your breast, / Infinities of love.*
—Laurence Hope (1865–1904), "Khan Zada's Song on the Hillside"

Central India's Chandela kings (the ninth to the twelfth centuries) built this compound of sacred temples in a forested area of Khajuraho. A few temples venerate Jain deities, but the majority honor Hindu deities—among them the gods Brahma, Vishnu, and Shiva and the goddess Devi Jagadambi. The stone shrines are richly embellished with carvings, many of them erotic scenes symbolizing the Divine male and female principles, a holy tribute to love and life.

Come to this spectacular World Heritage site if you desire to deepen your Divine love and to balance your worldly life with your inner spiritual life. Take a flight from Delhi, Agra, or Jaipur to Khajuraho's airport, or travel by train through the scenic Vindhya Range to Jhansi or Satna (the nearest stations) and then take a bus or cab to the temple complex.

Soothe Your Spirit

Stroll through the temples, being fully present to thoughts and feelings evoked by the sacred images. Meditate and pray, inviting love and compassion into your soul.

A Deeper Look

The Temples at Khajuraho—built from yellow, pink, and buff sandstone between A.D. 950 and 1050—represent the highest level of achievement in medieval Indian architecture. About twenty of the eighty-five temples remain extant.

Temppeliaukio Kirkko (Rock Church)◗
Helsinki, Finland

With this faith we will be able to hew out of the
mountain of despair a stone of hope.
—Martin Luther King Jr. (1929–1968), American clergyman and civil rights leader

The Rock Church, looking a bit like a Neolithic tomb recast into a modern architectural structure, was cut from bedrock in the middle of a residential area in 1968 by brothers and architects Timo and Tuomo Suomalainen. The exterior of this underground Lutheran church reveals only a portion of its dome-shaped copper roof, doing little to prepare first-time visitors for the bold interior: an astonishing circular sanctuary of rough-hewn rock walls bathed in natural light, a copper wire ceiling, a copper balcony, and dark wood furnishings with fuchsia cushions.

If you are inspired by images and sensations of strength, both tangible and intangible, visit Rock Church in the Etu-Töölö (southern district) of Helsinki. Take a tram from the city's main station and exit at the Sammonkatu stop.

Soothe Your Spirit

Attend a musical concert in this church (the acoustics are phenomenal), perhaps during the Easter or Christmas season. Cradled securely within the massive rock structure, feel the grounding strength of God's love and let the powerful sound of voices raised in fervent song connect you more firmly to your purpose.

A Deeper Look

The Rock Church has a structural collar (connecting the rock wall with the dome roof) that holds 180 vertical windows, allowing in natural light.

The Abbaye de Notre-Dame-de-Sénanque (Abbey of Sénanque) ◕

Gordes, Provence, France

Faith has to do with things that are not seen,
and hope with things that are not at hand.
—Saint Thomas Aquinas (1225–1274), Italian Christian theologian and philosopher

After French noblemen donated land in the valley north of the medieval village of Gordes in Provence for a monastery, Cistercian monks took up residence and built a simple sanctuary. Consecrated in 1178, the abbey endured centuries of turmoil, occupancy, abandonment, and reclamation. Today, Cistercian monks again occupy the honey-colored stone monastery nestled amid rolling hills of aromatic lavender bordered by a forest of fragrant pine.

Whether you seek the comfort of a heaven-scented spiritual retreat or the sheltering walls of a humble monastery, visit the Abbey of Sénanque. Visitors may attend services, which are posted at the entrance. Go in June or early July, when the lavender is in full bloom and before farmers begin harvesting. From Gordes, take D177 road approximately 2 miles.

Soothe Your Spirit

Book a retreat and bring along some spiritual books. As you explore the abbey, tune in to the sounds of monks as they perform a Gregorian chant. Walk to the cloister in the enclosed courtyard, taking in nature's scents and scenes. Settle into a quiet place and read for a while, and then meditate for deeper understanding of what you've read and experienced.

A Deeper Look

This abbey is one of the medieval Romanesque Cistercian monasteries known as the "Three Sisters of Provence." The others are Thoronet Abbey and Silvacane Abbey. For a guided tour, the fee is 7.50 euros.

The Abbaye de Notre-Dame-de-Sénanque
(Abbey of Sénanque), Gordes, Provence, France

The Asclepeion of Kos ◉

Kos, Greece

The art of healing comes from nature, not from the physician.
Therefore the physician must start from nature, with an open mind.
—Philippus Aureolus Paracelsus (1493–1541),
German-Swiss physician, botanist, and alchemist

When the ancient Greeks needed healing, they would visit a temple of Asclepius (god of healing) much as people today go to a medical clinic. The lovely island of Kos, located in the Dodecanese chain of islands in the Aegean Sea off the Asia Minor coast, is home to the well-preserved ruins of the Asclepeion of Kos, covering three terraces. The island is also the birthplace of Hippocrates, the Greek "Father of Medicine."

Whether you seek healing for yourself or someone else, visit the sacred ruins of Kos. Walk or ride a bicycle the nearly flat 3 miles from the nearest town (Kos), enjoying the scenery and serenity the moderate exercise provides, or take a bus.

Soothe Your Spirit

Bring your journal. Pray for healing before going to sleep at night, and then write your dreams in your journal when you awake. As you walk through the ruins, contemplate the curative message the Divine delivered to you in your dreams.

A Deeper Look

Ancient Greeks and Romans believed that Asclepius, the healing god, would appear in the patient's dream to cure him or her. People would sleep in an Asclepius temple and the next morning report their dreams to a priest, who would prescribe a cure.

The Baths of Caracalla⬤

Rome, Italy

*Health is the soul that animates all the enjoyments
of life, which fade and are tasteless without it.*
—Seneca (5 B.C.–A.D. 65), Roman dramatist, philosopher, and politician

This spectacular ruin in Rome was once a massive public bathing and entertainment complex constructed in the early third century A.D. The Baths of
Caracalla reflect the fundamentals of good health promoted by Roman phy-
sicians: bathing, exercise, relaxation, and a good diet. The complex included
a cafeteria, gymnasiums, a swimming pool, entertainment facilities, massage
areas, two saunas, and three types of pools (tepid, hot, cold) seating 1,600
bathers. This ancient health spa was used until A.D. 537, when Witigis besieged
Rome and destroyed the aqueducts supplying water to the site.

If you are intrigued with the connection between spiritual and physical
well-being, you will be inspired by the Baths of Caracalla. Take Metro Line B to
Circo Massimo Station; the ruins are at Viale delle Terme di Caracalla, south of
the Colosseum.

Soothe Your Spirit

Walk around the baths and reflect
on how improving your physical and
mental health might enhance or work
in harmony with your spiritual pursuits.

A Deeper Look

Over the centuries, priceless artwork
was plundered from the site, including
mosaics of athletes that covered the
gymnasium walls and are now in the
Vatican Museum, and a statue of a
muscular Hercules that, along with
other statues taken from the baths,
is in the archaeological museum of
Naples.

The Catacombs of Saint Callixtus⬤
Rome, Italy

Precious in the sight of the Lord is the death of his saints.
—Bible, Psalm 116:15

First established for Rome's early Christian community, the Catacombs of Saint Callixtus hold almost half a million sepulchers and tombs spanning 12 miles and five levels. Saint Cecilia was martyred with three ax chops to her neck in the third century and is entombed where a statue marks the place of her burial. Her relics were moved to a basilica dedicated to her in the Trastevere, along with forty-six other martyrs; and the Crypt of the Popes is the oldest.

If holy burial sites depicting ancient Christians' spiritual beliefs and their sacred art and symbols inspire you to create a rich spiritual life for yourself, visit the Catacombs of Saint Callixtus. The catacomb address is Via Appia Antica (Old Appian Way), 110/126, Rome; the entrance is located near the small church of Quo Vadis and the Basilica of Saint Sebastian, with parking off Via Ardeatina. To reach the catacombs, take the metro, your rental car, taxi, coach tour, or any of various city buses that depart from central Rome.

Photography is not permitted inside the catacombs.

Soothe Your Spirit
Tap into your artistic self and draw the beautiful symbols you see. Later, your images will carry you back to what you saw and felt in the catacombs. Use the emotion to lead you into prayer, meditation, and absorption on the Divine.

A Deeper Look
The catacombs bear the name of early Christian deacon Callixtus, administrator of the cemeteries of the Church of Rome through appointment by Pope Zephyrinus early in the third century.

The Cave of the Apocalypse⬥
Pátmos, Greece

Write the things which thou hast seen, and the things which are,
and the things which shall be hereafter...
—Bible, Revelation 1:19

When Roman emperor Domitian exiled Saint John the Divine in A.D. 95 to Pátmos, an arid Greek island sandwiched between Fourni, Leros, and Ikaria in the Dodecanese chain, the saint took refuge in a cave on a rocky hill and began to dictate his astonishing dreams and apocalyptic visions to his disciple Prohoros. The cave became the Cave of the Apocalypse and the words became the Revelation of Saint John the Divine, the last book of the New Testament.

Whether you desire a rejuvenation of your spiritual life or a total spiritual transformation, come to Pátmos and sit in the cave. Take a hydrofoil plane from the airports on Samos, Kos, or Leros or catch the ferry from Piraeus—a nine- to ten-hour trip to Pátmos. It is possible to take the ferry from other islands of the eastern Aegean or Dodecanese chains. Reach the cave on foot from Skala (a bit of walk), catch one of the buses that follow regular routes through the villages, or drive your rental car.

Soothe Your Spirit

Sit on a bench inside the cave, close your eyes, and open your heart. Let the energy of this holy place transform you, rejuvenating your spirit and filling your heart with Divine love.

A Deeper Look

Guides will tell you about what to see in the cave: icons, rock formations, niches, droplets of ancient water sealed inside volcanic rock. However, tourists and pilgrims are welcome to sit, pray, and meditate.

The Church of All Nations✸
Jerusalem, Israel

And they came to a place which was named Gethsemane:
and he saith to his disciples, Sit ye here, while I shall pray...
—Bible, Mark 14:32–36

When Jesus was in the Garden of Gethsemane with his disciples before his arrest, he told them to sit while he walked off a short distance to pray. Today, the Church of All Nations, also known as the Basilica of the Agony, sits upon the site where Jesus prayed, and the sacred piece of bedrock upon which he prayed is enshrined in the church.

If you desire to cultivate the kind of spiritual strength that Christ exemplified, see the basilica that numerous nations helped build. Located at the base of the Mount of Olives, the Garden of Gethsemane is on many Jerusalem walking tours and is easy to reach by rental car or taxi.

Soothe Your Spirit
Reflect on the agony Jesus felt as he prayed. Notice the purplish-blue alabaster used in the basilica's windows to evoke a somber mood, indicative of Christ's agony even as he accepted God's will. Think of three ways you could work on developing that kind of spiritual resolve.

A Deeper Look
The Church of All Nations was built on a site once occupied by a fourth-century B.C. basilica that toppled in an earthquake and a twelfth-century Crusader chapel. The modern church was consecrated in 1924.

The First Church of Christ, Scientist (The Mother Church) ∾

Boston, Massachusetts, United States

Health is not a condition of matter, but of Mind.
—Mary Baker Eddy (1821–1910), founder of the Christian Science movement

When Mary Baker Eddy read a story about a miraculous healing performed by Jesus, she experienced an epiphany and became cured of her own disability, which inspired her to found the Christian Science movement, with its emphasis on faith healing and Jesus' healing works. The Mother Church, as this first church of the movement is called, is an architectural gem, built in the Romanesque Revival style with a later Renaissance-style extension featuring a gorgeous Byzantine-style dome. The plaza features a peaceful reflecting pool and fountain.

If you would like to learn more about the physical and moral healing practices and beliefs of the Christian Scientists, visit the Mother Church and its eleven-story library. Located in Boston's Back Bay neighborhood, it is easily reached by car or public transportation, including buses and the subway.

Soothe Your Spirit

Attend a Bible lesson-sermon by lay readers (there are no ordained ministers) and listen to hymns. Allow enough time to tour this lovely and large old church, soaking up its healing energy and letting it work its magic on you.

A Deeper Look

The First Church of Christ, Scientist that subsequently spawned 1,700 branch churches and societies has an amazing Aeolian-Skinner pipe organ that is several stories high, one of the largest in the United States.

The First Church of Christ, Scientist (The Mother Church), Boston, Massachusetts, United States

The Golden Temple✳

Amritsar, Punjab, India

Give up your selfishness, and you shall find peace;
like water mingling with water, you shall merge in absorption.
—Sri Guru Granth Sahib

The Sri Harmandir Sahib, or Golden Temple, is the holiest, most exquisite shrine in the Sikh religion with elaborate gold gilding and white marble walls, precious stone floral inlay, and richly patterned floors. Its atmosphere of reverence and devotion befits a sacred sanctuary whose name means "abode of God." Sitting on an island surrounded by the Amrit Sarovar (Pool of Immortal Holy Nectar), the temple houses the eternal spirit of the Sikh founder, Guru Nanak, who preached that spiritual enlightenment could be achieved through meditation on God's name.

To appease your spiritual hunger or to find deeper meaning in your spiritual life, visit the Temple. Take a flight into Amritsar International Airport, and then a bus, a taxi, or a cycle-rickshaw to the temple. Allow several hours to explore the compound and the Temple of God (Hari Mandir), beautifully adorned with verses from the Sikh's holiest book, the Guru Granth Sahib.

Remove your shoes and wash your feet in the wading pool before entering the temple. Dress respectfully and cover your head (scarves are provided). Do not consume alcohol, cigarettes, or meat while on the premises. Photography is not permitted inside the shrine.

Soothe Your Spirit

Read a sacred verse at random from the *Guru Granth Sahib*, considered the living embodiment of the Sikh gurus and their sacred teachings. Contemplate the deeper meaning of the verse and let it guide you through your day.

A Deeper Look

Construction of the temple began in 1574 and was completed in 1604 when the holy book was installed. The temple was designed with four entrances to symbolize Sikh's welcome and acceptance of all who enter.

The House of Peter✪
Capernaum, Galilee, Israel

And Jesus walking by the sea of Galilee, saw two brethren, Simon called Peter, and Andrew his brother, casting a net into the sea: for they were fishers. And he saith unto them, Follow me, and I will make you fishers of men.
—Bible, Matthew 4:18–19

Capernaum, a small fishing village on the coast of the Sea of Galilee, was home to brothers Peter and Andrew who worked in their father's fishing business until called by Jesus to become fishers of men. In modern times, Franciscans built an octagonal church with a glass viewing platform over Peter's house, which is said to be the place where Jesus healed Peter's mother-in-law of a fever, cured a paralytic lowered through the roof, and stayed when in the area.

If seeing this holy site would help you release something or give you hope, come to the House of Peter. Capernaum is about 9 miles from Tiberius, capital of Galilee, and is easily reachable by car or bus from Tiberius. Visit the site as a self-guided day trip, or with a guide or as part of a bus tour.

Soothe Your Spirit
Make a vow at the holy site affirming what you want to release. Later, put some grains of salt into your palm and mentally repeat the statement of release before tossing the salt away.

A Deeper Look
Peter's house is situated near an ancient home church with writing about Jesus in Aramaic, Latin, Greek, and Syriac on the wall, as well as references to Peter in graffiti.

The Saadian Tombs⊕
Marrakesh, Morocco

There is no God but God. Muhammad is God's messenger.
—Qur'an

Perhaps the most beautiful burial sites in North Africa are the tombs of the Saadian sultans and their families, who ruled in the sixteenth and seventeenth centuries. The tombs, buried for centuries, were rediscovered and restored in 1917 by the Beaux-arts service. The sacred site (next door to the Mosque of the Kasbah) continues to be a place of veneration. Some tombs are embellished in gorgeous mosaics and epitaphs, while others are housed inside two mausoleums with richly decorated rooms, pillared arches, stunning patterned floors and domed ceilings, Arabic script, and amazing plaster work.

If funerary art provides solace to you during your time of loss or is spiritually evocative, visit the tombs. Located on Rue de la Kasbah Marrakesh, the site is easily accessible via the international airport and through regular bus and train service from other Moroccan cities. Arrive early to avoid long lines of tourists. Entrance fee is 6 euros. Hours are 9:00 a.m. to 5:00 p.m.

Soothe Your Spirit
Allow the art and subtle spiritual energy of this tranquil, sacred site to magnify the longing in your heart for God's love.

A Deeper Look
The Saadian Tombs lie in an enclosed garden of roses in Marrakesh's old Medina. Sultan Ahmad al-Mansur (1578–1603), who oversaw the design and construction of the tombs, is buried here, along with 166 to 200 others.

The Saadian Tombs, Marrakesh, Morocco

The Sacred Garden❋
Lumbini, Nepal

On life's journey faith is nourishment, virtuous deeds are a shelter,
wisdom is the light by day and right mindedness is the protection
by night. If a man lives a pure life, nothing can destroy him.
—Siddhartha Gautama, the Buddha (563–483 B.C.), father of Buddhism

As a small boy, Buddha likely played in the shade of the beautiful sal trees (Shorea robusta), which grew in the tranquil gardens of the Kolias and Shakya clans of Lumbini. His father, King Suddhodana, belonged to the Shakya clan. Situated near the Sacred Garden is the famous Ashoka pillar, which bears the inscription identifying this sacred site as the birthplace of Buddha.

If you seek the spiritual protection of the Buddha in the way that he sought spiritual shelter through introspection and meditation, come to the Sacred Garden. Even if you don't, visit Lumbini to experience his enlightening presence; the Buddha dictated that the four holy places of Buddhism would include his birthplace. Lumbini is located roughly 15.5 miles east of Kapilavastu.

Soothe Your Spirit
Sit under the sal tree that, according to legend, gave support and protection to Maya Devi, the Buddha's mother, who is said to have reached up and clutched its branch while in labor with her son.

A Deeper Look
Recent excavation in the Sacred Garden uncovered a stone with the imprint of a foot that is believed to mark the exact spot of the Buddha's birth.

The United States Memorial Holocaust Museum●
Washington, DC, United States

In Italy, the country where fascism was born, we have a particular relation with the Holocaust, but as a turning point in history, it belongs to everybody in the world. It is a part of humanity.
—Roberto Benigni (1952–), Academy Award–winning Italian actor, comedian, and filmmaker

Designed by Holocaust survivor and architect James Ingo Freed, the interior spaces of this structure and exhibits are created to be a "resonator of memory," meaning that careful thought has been given so that the interior spaces allude to some aspect of the Holocaust, as uncomfortable, terrifying, and solemn as that is for visitors. This is not a sacred sanctuary in the usual sense but rather a haunting place that can deeply touch the spiritual core of those who visit. The museum optimizes the use of hard, cold, impersonal surfaces, spaces, and exhibits to unfold a narrative about our inhumanity to fellow human beings.

Whether you carry some darkness in your heart that blocks your spiritual light or vision, take time to visit the United States Memorial Holocaust Museum, for it has lessons for all of us on forgiveness, reconciliation, and redemption. Use the blue, orange, and silver metro lines to get to the museum located at 100 Raoul Wallenberg Place SW. Walk west after getting off at the Smithsonian stop.

Soothe Your Spirit
Give yourself time to process your feelings as you work your way through the exhibits. Be cognizant of the opposites of dark and light, despair and hope, for this double-sided Janus face is present throughout. Pray for the elimination of those things that cause division and aggression and intolerance in humanity. Pray for healing.

A Deeper Look
The priceless collections of Holocaust-related materials housed in the museum have been amassed from all over the world and organized into eight groupings.

The Valley of the Kings⊕
Luxor, Egypt

He who cannot change the very fabric of his thought
will never be able to change reality...
—Anwar Sadat (1918–1981), third president of Egypt

When the ancient Egyptians said goodbye to a king, he was sent into the afterlife with jewels, ritual sacred objects, statues of deities, furniture, and scrolls; that is why tomb robbing was such a lucrative practice. Ramses XI, who reigned from 1124 B.C. until his death in 1106 B.C., was the last king to build a tomb in the valley. His simple tomb is vibrantly colored with scenes from the *Book of the Dead* and other ancient texts.

If you are facing the end of a karmic cycle and must say goodbye to someone or something, it might help to see how the ancient Egyptians handled death. The Valley of the Kings is on the west bank of the Nile; from Luxor, take a taxi or a rental car approximately 4 miles upriver. Alternatively, cross the river on a ferry. The coolest months to visit are December through March. Otherwise, daytime temperatures reach triple digits.

Buy your tickets at the West Bank ticket office since you cannot purchase tickets at the site. Women must cover bare shoulders and knees.

Soothe Your Spirit
Formulate a ritual for achieving closure (when you return home); for example, write a note saying goodbye. Cut it into pieces and plant it in a pot with some forget-me-nots. Or, if you want a permanent ending, write the note and burn it.

A Deeper Look
The tomb has been open since antiquity; more than a dozen messages of graffiti were left in the tomb by ancient tourists.

The Western (Wailing) Wall⊛

Jerusalem, Israel

He who has not seen the Temple of Herod,
has never seen a beautiful building.
—Babylonian Talmud, Baba Batra, 4a; Shemot Rabba 36:1

Since the destruction of the Second Temple of Herod in A.D. 70, Jews have been coming to the only remnant of the temple—a section of stone wall that surrounded the complex—to lament and pray. The Western Wall, popularly known as the Wailing Wall, is the holiest Judaic site in the world, attracting more than eight million Jews and non-Jews annually. Today, the wall looks like God's message board, with notes containing prayers stuffed into the cracks.

If you wish to release your pain to God and open your heart to Divine love and compassion, visit Jerusalem to pray and reflect before the Wailing Wall. Go to the section designated for your gender (women and men pray in separate areas, according to Jewish Orthodox practice), and dress appropriately. Near the entrance, you can find head coverings for men and shawls and skirt coverings for women.

Soothe Your Spirit

Write your prayer on a slip of paper and tuck it into the sacred wall or take it home in a beautiful piece of Middle Eastern pottery that you designate as a prayer receptacle.

A Deeper Look

The site of the Western Wall has been sacred since the first Judaic temple of Jerusalem was built there five thousand years ago. Jews believe that God resides in the Western Wall and that praying there gives the supplicant the strongest earthly connection with the Divine.

Thian Hock Keng Temple (Temple of Heavenly Bliss)✲

Singapore, Republic of Singapore

Being deeply loved by someone gives you strength,
while loving someone gives you courage.
—Lao Tzu (600–531 B.C.), Chinese philosopher and father of Taoism

The Thian Hock Keng Temple honors both Mazu, Taoist goddess of the sailors and fishermen, and Kuan Yin, the Buddhist bodhisattva of mercy and compassion. The temple serves as a reminder to visitors of the Chinese immigrants who prayed to Mazu for safe passage. Built in 1839 on the site of a joss house, it reflects the ornate Chinese temple–style with its square shape, crenulated roof, and stone threshold.

If you seek Divine protection for a journey, visit the Thian Hock Keng Temple at 158 Telok Ayer Street. Walk from Raffles Place or the Tanjong Pagar MTR station. The nearest airport offering international service is the Singapore Changi Airport.

Soothe Your Spirit

Write a prayer on a piece of paper to burn in the red kiln in the courtyard for good luck.

A Deeper Look

The statue of Confucius sits inside one pagoda, and sacred ancestral tablets of the temple's founders are in the other pagoda.

Tikal☯

Tikal National Park, El Petén, Guatemala

The Track of the Sun / across the Sky / leaves its shining message, /
Illuminating, / Strengthening, / Warming, / us who are here, /
showing us we are not alone...
—Atoni; Choctaw Native American blessing

Tikal, built in 600 B.C., was one of the most powerful kingdoms in Meso-america. The towering 230-foot limestone temples left behind when the Maya people abandoned Tikal by the tenth century are monuments to the glory of their civilization at its peak. Archaeologists have found dozens of pyramids, some with stone implements that amplify the human voice, possibly enabling spiritual leaders to speak with godlike intonation from the top of the pyramids.

If you seek spiritual strength to empower your voice or message, visit Tikal. Book a guided tour at the site, near the museum. Fly from Guatemala City to Flores (on Lake Petén Itzá) and drive an hour to Tikal. From San Ignacio in Belize, Tikal is a two-hour drive.

Soothe Your Spirit

Climb to the top of a pyramid and offer a prayer for strength or a mantra affirming your great faith to the Divine. Let the words rise slowly from your heart to the top of your throat, out of your mouth, onto the wind, and toward the sun.

A Deeper Look

The abundant wildlife of Petén and the archaeological significance of the site prompted UNESCO to signify Tikal as both a Natural and a Cultural World Heritage site.

Tiwanaku (Tiahuanaco)⊕
La Paz, Bolivia

...Be still until the sunlight pours through and dispels the mists /
as it surely will / Then act with courage.
—White Eagle (1800s–1914), Ponca chief

Tiwanaku, the sacred ruins of a pre-Columbian religious and political center in the Bolivian highlands, is surrounded by mountains on three sides and a lake on the fourth, features the ancients believed had protective and spiritual qualities. Prehistoric Andean people occupied this powerful city-state from A.D. 300 to 1000, when they suddenly disappeared. Five hundred years later, the sun-worshipping Incas laid claim to the abandoned city, which they believed was the birthplace of the Inca people and a gateway to their many gods. Purportedly a nexus for spiritual energy, Tiwanaku continues to be sacred to Andean people and now draws New Age devotees, scholars, and tourists from around the globe.

If you desire strength to endure adversity, make a pilgrimage to this sacred place high in the Andes (13,000 feet above sea level) that has endured for fourteen thousand years. Reach Tiwanaku by bus from La Paz, Bolivia's capital city, or take a guided coach tour.

Soothe Your Spirit
Join the thousands who come in June for the summer solstice. Dress warmly and find a spot with a good vista and good energy. As you watch the sun rise, feel the exhilaration rise in your soul and thank the Creator for the life-giving rays that warm your body.

A Deeper Look
Viracocha, the god of action, is one of many deities the Inca associated with Tiwanaku, now a World Heritage site.

NO PASAR
NO PASS

Tiwanaku (Tiahuanaco), La Paz, Bolivia

Tomba di Giganti di Coddu Vecchiu⬣

Arzachena, Sardinia, Italy

Great griefs are mute.
—Italian proverb

The people of the ancient Nuragic civilization on Sardinia during the Bronze Age produced sacred megalithic tombs of astonishing size, including the giant tomb of Coddu Vecchiu, with its 33-foot-long burial chamber and a semi-circular area in front where sacred ceremonies for the dead were performed. The later addition of the giant stele (large, upright carved stone) connects this tomb with other megalithic tombs found across Europe.

If you are having difficulty finding closure over a personal loss and would like to feel rejuvenated, visit the Tomb of Coddu Vecchiu to gain perspective about the cycles of birth and death and the rise and fall of civilizations. The main airport is Olbia Costa Smeralda. There are daily passenger ferries from Italy to Olbia as well as two rail networks that will get you from cities on Sardinia to Olbia. From Olbia, take a local bus to Arzachena or take the main road (SS 125) to Arzachena. The gigantic tomb sits in the southwestern area of Arzachena known as Capichera.

Soothe Your Spirit

Pay your respects to the ancient spirits. Sit near the tomb, breathe deeply, and relax before intuitively attuning to the energy of this sacred place. According to a prevailing belief, this site rejuvenates those who come in contact with it. Let it revitalize you, help you gain perspective, and find closure.

A Deeper Look

There are 321 megalithic monuments across Sardinia, including the Tomba di Giganti di Coddu Vecchiu, which archaeologists suggest was most likely a community burial chamber.

Tulum ☯
Yucatán, Mexico

Tell me who you live with and I will tell you who you are.
—Hispanic proverb

The once-jungle-covered late-Mayan city of Tulum stands on a cliff over-looking a white powder beach stretching along the sparkling blue Carib-bean Sea, like a sacred gift from the gods to whom the Maya prayed for boun-tiful crops, healthy families, and good marriages. The temples, sanctuaries, and offertories of the Tulum ruins, once a place of worship for Maya kings, provide a view into their civilization, when family and friendship were as important to the ancient Maya as they are to their descendants.

If you want to share a spiritually enriching experience with your spouse or to take a solitary retreat in order to gain perspective on a personal relationship, come to Tulum. From Cancún, take a bus, rental car, tour package, or hired car and driver. Allow two hours to get there and a few hours to see everything.

Soothe Your Spirit

Walk around the ruins, soaking up the peaceful beauty and spiritual energy of this sacred site. Climb the steep steps to the top of the main temple; sit in quiet meditation or prayer. Later, go for a refreshing swim.

A Deeper Look

Tulum has three areas: Tulum Pueblo (the town, with markets, hostels, hotels, restaurants, etc.), Tulum Playa (the beach area and ecology reserve), and Tulum Ruins (the archaeological site); none are within walking distance of each other. The ruin is the third most visited archaeological site in Mexico.

Ulun Danu Bratan Temple⦿

Lake Bratan, Bali, Indonesia

Water is life's mater and matrix, mother and medium.
There is no life without water.
—Albert Szent-Györgyi (1893–1986), Hungarian chemist and Nobel laureate

Ulun Danu Bratan (also Beratan) Temple in Bali's Bedugul highlands is a stunning water temple situated on a shimmering lake surrounded by malachite green hills and thickly forested mountains frequently shrouded in mist. The temple takes its name from Dewi Danu (goddess of the lake), the source of fertility and prosperity, and from Lake Bratan, which nourishes life by irrigating rice fields throughout Bali. Inside the sanctuary of this important Buddhist-Hindu temple with its multilevel pagoda shape (Meru) is a shrine dedicated to Brahma (the Creator) and a smaller temple honoring Dewi Bhogawati, goddess of food and drink.

If you prefer sacred sanctuary in a fecund natural setting, visit Ulun Danu Bratan Temple. Getting there means traveling from south to north on a road that lifts gently through rice fields, terraces, and cocoa plantations, affording lovely coastal views. At certain times of the year, local people come to the temple to pray and receive blessings.

Soothe Your Spirit

This is not a public temple, and since tourists and nonmembers are not allowed inside the temple, head for the lake's edge past the manicured gardens, stopping to meditate before the stunning Buddhist stupa (bell-shaped tower) along the way. Alternately, arrange for a small boat to take you out on the lake to view the temple at dawn, and pray or perhaps perform a fertility ritual.

A Deeper Look

Built in 1633 by the Raja (Hindu king) Mengwi, the temple is now a World Heritage site.

Ulun Danu Bratan Temple, Lake Bratan, Bali, Indonesia

Uluru ✺
Northern Territory, Australia

Those who stop dreaming are lost.
—Aboriginal proverb

U luru, or Ayers Rock, rises seemingly out of nowhere in the flat southern section of Australia's Northern Territory. The oval-shaped sandstone formation is a magnificent natural creation, climbing more than 1,100 feet high with a circumference of almost 6 miles. Adding to the wonder, the massive monolith appears to change colors depending on the time of day and time of year, even looking as if it glows red at sunrise and sunset.

A sacred site of the Aboriginal people, Uluru is surrounded by springs and rock caves adorned with ancient paintings. Located about 200 miles southwest of Alice Springs, it is virtually in the center of the country. You can either fly directly into Ayers Rock Airport or into Alice Springs Airport and take a breathtaking ride on the Red Centre Way.

Soothe Your Spirit

As you explore the area around Uluru and take in its beauty, reflect on the many souls who have walked the same path around the formation and the many who will walk in your footsteps in the future.

A Deeper Look

While climbing this World Heritage site is not prohibited, the Aboriginal people have asked visitors to respect their culture and not climb the formation. There are also certain areas around Uluru where you're asked not to take photographs. Be mindful and respectful during your visit.

Umayyad Mosque
(Great Mosque of Damascus) ✲
Damascus, Syria

And your Lord said, "Invoke me. I will respond..."
—Qur'an, 40:60

B efore this triumph of Islamic mosques was built in A.D. 705, the land on which it stands held a succession of sacred structures. First, there was an Aramaic temple to Hadad, which gave way to a Roman temple exalting Jupiter. In the fourth century B.C., Byzantines converted the temple into a church, which, after the fall of Damascus in A.D. 661, they shared with Muslim worshippers: Christians on the west, Muslims on the east. By 670, the Christians had moved into Saint John the Baptist Cathedral nearby. The small church was stripped of its Roman and Byzantine features, and construction of the great mosque ensued.

Umayyad Mosque stands today as the ultimate in Islamic mosque design; it is artistically superior, with a large domed nave and an open courtyard with three porticos. Among the 777 monuments enshrined in this great mosque are one of the three original copies of the Qur'an and the relics of Saint John the Baptist.

Whether you wish to seek guidance from Allah or to see one of Islam's most important places of worship, visit Umayyad Mosque. Fly into Damascus International Airport and take a taxi to the mosque in the Old City section of Damascus. Observe all Islamic customs.

Soothe Your Spirit
Pray, asking Allah for the spiritual succor you seek.

A Deeper Look
One of the mosque's minarets is believed to be the passage through which Jesus (Issa) will return to Earth.

Waipoua Forest ⊗

Northland Region, New Zealand

Love received demands love returned.
—Māori proverb

The Waipoua Forest, located in northern New Zealand, captures the beauty of the country's lush landscape. The sanctuary helps to preserve the magnificent kauri trees, which hold a special place in Māori lore. It is within Waipoua Forest that the largest known kauri tree, Tāne Mahuta, stands at almost 150 feet tall with a girth of just over 50 feet. This picturesque natural reserve is the perfect place to visit to get back in touch with nature and commune with the giant trees.

If you are looking to experience New Zealand's natural beauty, you can head up the west coast of the Northland Region. You're able to explore the park on your own or sign up for a guided tour. While impressive at all hours of the day, you may want to consider signing up for an evening tour with a local guide.

Soothe Your Spirit

Enjoy forest bathing as you explore the area, honoring your connection with nature and appreciating the natural beauty that has been thriving for thousands of years. Tāne Mahuta is believed to be between 1,250 and 2,500 years old.

A Deeper Look

According to the Māori creation myth, Tāne Mahuta is the son of Ranginui, the sky father, and Papatūānuku, the earth mother. Tāne broke his parents' marital embrace and separated them in order to give him and his siblings space to live.

Wat Phra Kaew
(Temple of the Emerald Buddha)✹
Bangkok, Thailand

We have more possibilities available in each moment than we realize.
—Thich Nhat Hanh (1926–), exiled Vietnamese Buddhist
monk, scholar, poet, and peace activist

The holiest *wat* in Thailand, the Temple of the Emerald Buddha is situated on the Grand Palace grounds in Bangkok's historic center (Phra Nakhon) and safeguards a seated Buddha carved out of a single green stone (jasper) and dating back six centuries. The 2-foot-tall Buddha—a talisman of prosperity and protection for the Thai people—can only be touched by the Thai king when he changes the icon's gold garments at the heart of Thailand's three seasons (hot, rainy, cold).

If you wish to attract abundance into your life, visit Wat Phra Kaew. Take a taxi or *tuk-tuk* (a three-wheel auto taxi) or walk to the site. There is a fee for non-Thai visitors. Photography inside is forbidden. Dress appropriately (no revealing clothing) and remove your shoes. When praying, do not point your feet toward the Emerald Buddha.

Soothe Your Spirit
Allow at least two hours at the temple and the Grand Palace to soak up the palpable peace that seems to emanate from this holy place. Make an offering, light a stick of incense, and meditate on the Divine provider and protector.

A Deeper Look
According to legend, the Emerald Buddha was created by the Indian sculptor and Buddhist sage Nagasena in 43 B.C. to bring prosperity, protection, and preeminence to the kingdom (country) in which it resides. The icon came to Thailand in A.D. 1432 by way of Cambodia and before that Laos (fifth century), after spending three hundred years in its birthplace, Patna, India.

Wat Phra Kaew (Temple of the Emerald Buddha), Bangkok, Thailand

Winchester Cathedral◓
Winchester, Hampshire, England

Finally, be strong in the Lord and in the strength of his might.
—Bible, Ephesians 6:10

When Saint Swithun (Swithin), Anglo-Saxon bishop of Winchester and zealous builder and renovator of churches, died in A.D. 862, he was buried in the open—as he had adamantly instructed—between the Old Minster church and Saint Martin's Tower. A decade later, when an attempt was made to move his remains inside the church, legend has it that the saint caused it to rain for forty days, thus prohibiting his reburial. In 1093, the saint's relics were successfully transferred into Winchester Cathedral. Constructed of limestone that dazzles in the sunlight, this Romanesque sanctuary features soaring spires, flying buttresses, fourteen splendid church bells, and the longest nave (556 feet) of any cathedral in England.

Visit glorious Winchester Cathedral to pray for the spiritual conviction of Saint Swithun on July 15 (his feast day), throughout August when the weather is best (but the crowds are large), or at Christmas to hear the empowering chorale music.

Soothe Your Spirit
Reflect on the "raindrops" in your life and pray for the courage, patience, and perseverance to overcome them.

A Deeper Look
A popular pilgrimage site, especially during the Middle Ages, Winchester Cathedral venerates the Holy Trinity as well as Saints Peter, Paul, and Swithun. It safeguards the relics of numerous Saxon kings, members of the clergy, and writer Jane Austen in addition to those of Saint Swithun.

Yosemite Chapel◖

Yosemite National Park, Northern California, United States

The clearest way into the universe is through a forested wilderness.
—John Muir (1838–1914), Scottish-born American naturalist

After the National Sunday School Assembly raised enough funds in dona-tions, mostly from schoolchildren, construction began on a small New England–style church with a single spire in 1879. Although it has been moved from its original location near the Four Mile Trail, Yosemite Chapel, the oldest constructed structure in Yosemite National Park, sits in a picturesque area of Yosemite Valley with awe-inspiring views of gorgeous wilderness. Spectacular waterfalls, verdant forests, astonishing cliffs, giant sequoias, and breathtaking-ly beautiful mountain peaks stir the spirit beyond comprehension.

If you long for renewal by communing with the Divine in the beauty of nature or in an exquisite natural setting, visit the chapel in Yosemite. By car or coach, take Highway 120 or California State Highways 41 or 140 to Yosemite National Park. Learn more at www.yosemitevalleychapel.org.

Highway 120 is subject to closure in the winter when Tioga Pass is impass-able (usually November though late May).

Soothe Your Spirit

In this chapel, vow to make your worship regular, joyous, and intimate, and then commune with the Divine often throughout the day(s) as you roam, hike, camp, and relax in this stunning natural setting.

A Deeper Look

Yosemite became a United States national park in 1890 and receives four million visitors each year (mainly during the summer). Half Dome, one of the peaks, rises 4,000 feet above the valley floor, making it a world-renowned landmark that visitors love to photograph.

INDEX

ABOUT THE AUTHOR

Meera Lester, an internationally published author, has written more than two dozen books, including *Rituals for Life*, *My Pocket Meditations*, *The Secret Power of You*, and *The Everything® Law of Attraction Book*. After spending time in India during her early twenties and later traveling to dozens of other countries, Meera developed a deep respect for the cultural and spiritual traditions of people throughout the world. She has been a lifelong practitioner of yoga, meditation, and prayer. She also writes mysteries and blogs about living in harmony with nature at HennyPennyFarmette.com.